Holy Week Services

Holy Week Services

Joint Liturgical Group

Revised and expanded edition
Edited by Donald Gray

Holy Week Services is a revised and expanded version
of a work of the same title published in 1971.

SPCK: The Society for Promoting Christian Knowledge
Holy Trinity Church, Marylebone Road, London NW1 4DU

British Library Cataloguing in Publication Data

Joint Liturgical Group
  Holy Week services (full edition)
  .—2nd ed., rev. and expanded
  1. Holy Week
  I. Title
  264′03   BX5147.H6

  ISBN 0–281–04039–7

Filmset in Monophoto Photina by
Northumberland Press Ltd, Gateshead
Printed in Great Britain by
Richard Clay (The Chaucer Press) Ltd
Bungay, Suffolk

CONTENTS

Members of the Joint Liturgical Group
1983

The Church of England
The Rev. Canon D. C. Gray, *Secretary*
Professor the Rev. Canon D. R. Jones

The Church of Scotland
The Rev. D. M. Beckett
The Rev. J. C. Stewart

The Baptist Union of Great Britain and Ireland
The Rev. N. Clark
The Rev. M. F. Williams

The United Reformed Church
The Rev. D. McIhagga
The Rev. Dr C. Thompson

The Methodist Church
The Rev. A. Raymond George
The Rev. Gordon S. Wakefield, *Chairman*

The Fellowship of the Churches of Christ
The Rev. H. Merritt

The Episcopal Church in Scotland
The Rev. Dr G. Tellini

The Roman Catholic Church
The Rev. E. Matthews
The Very Rev. Canon H. E. Winstone

Publications of the Joint Liturgical Group
established in 1963

The Renewal of Worship 1965 (OUP)
The Calendar and Lectionary 1967 (OUP)
The Daily Office 1968;
    10th corrected impression 1973 (SPCK and Epworth)
An Additional Lectionary 1969 (SPCK and Epworth)
Holy Week Services 1971 (SPCK and Epworth)
Initiation and Eucharist 1972 (SPCK)
Worship and the Child 1975 (SPCK)
The Daily Office Revised 1978 (SPCK)
Getting the Liturgy Right 1982 (SPCK)
Holy Week Services
   Revised and expanded edition 1983 (SPCK)

PREFACE

In recent years there has been an increasing desire in all the denominations to observe the days of Holy Week as special times of devotion. There is also a growing practice of making these occasions ecumenical.

The services in this book, particularly those for the Monday, Tuesday and Wednesday in Holy Week, can be used ecumenically but they are also intended as an offering to the Churches from the Joint Liturgical Group for use in their own denominational worship.

With both these uses in mind the Group has prepared a book which contains all that is needed for the conduct of the services rather than the skeletal outlines which were contained in our earlier booklet *Holy Week Services* published in 1971. At the same time there is available a shorter edition which we trust will enable the maximum congregational participation in these services. At the foot of each page on which a service begins, we give the corresponding page number in the shorter edition.

It is our hope that the results of our work will encourage the Churches to contemplate the power of the Cross to destroy our sinful self-satisfaction and realize that through the Resurrection of our Lord Jesus Christ we are all brought into the new life of peace and unity.

DONALD GRAY

ACKNOWLEDGEMENTS

The Scripture quotations in this publication are from the Revised Standard Version of the Bible, copyrighted 1946, 1952 © 1971, 1973 by the Division of Christian Education of the National Council of the Churches of Christ in the USA, and used by permission.

The psalms included are from *The Psalms : A New Translation for Worship* (The Liturgical Psalter) © 1976, 1977 English Text David L. Frost, John A. Emerton, Andrew A. Macintosh, by permission of William Collins Sons & Co. Ltd.

Thanks are also due to the following for permission to reproduce copyright material:

The Central Board of Finance of the Church of England: the Commandments (Holy Communion Rite A first version) and prayers from *The Alternative Service Book 1980*

International Committee on English in the Liturgy: adaptations of the Solemn Prayers and the Reproaches (Good Friday) and of the Easter Proclamation (The Easter Vigil)

Methodist Publishing House: extracts from The Covenant Service (*The Methodist Service Book*, 1975)

Geoffrey Chapman, a division of Cassell Ltd: the translation © 1969 James Quinn sj of *Ubi Caritas*, from the Latin Liturgy of Maundy Thursday

A. R. Mowbray and Co. Ltd: A Thanksgiving for the Resurrection from *Cambridge Offices and Orisons*, edited by E. Milner-White and B. T. D. Smith

Oxford University Press: the hymn 'Sing, my tongue, the glorious battle' (*English Hymnal* 95), verses translated by Percy Dearmer

HOLY WEEK

Gordon S. Wakefield

THE EVOLUTION OF HOLY WEEK

The observance of the week before Easter as a time of intensive Christian commemoration through a whole series of devout exercises redolent of the events of the Gospel, was not customary in the Church of the first three centuries. There are three strands which have gone to make the rich tapestry to which we are heirs. One of them has come to appear dominant, but the others are not completely obliterated, even now.

First is the belief that Christians already live in the age to come, that their baptism is their initiation into *the* new life,[1] and that they meet in their Lord's Day Assembly as citizens of the Kingdom of God, 'at the beginning of another world'.[2] The Eucharist would constantly remind them of what baptism had even more dramatically proclaimed, that the source of the new life is the death and resurrection of the Lord.

Second is the fact that the events thus symbolized and recalled took place at the time of the Jewish Passover. Early and inevitably that season evoked particular commemoration, though this was almost universally on the Sunday following the Passover, not on the day itself, and was not, at first, 'a reproduction of the successive events of the Passion and Resurrection on the several days of their occurrence'.[3] Suffering and victory were not separated into different acts of worship at different times. The Friday of the crucifixion was not observed as such. Everything was concentrated into the great Paschal Vigil of Holy Saturday – Easter Morning, which included the rites of initiation and the Easter Eucharist. This became the supreme occasion for baptism and the renewal of baptismal vows. It was preceded by the instruction in the faith which ended the two-year catechumenate and was prepared for also by a time of fasting. The period for this was gradually elongated until it became the season of forty days, which we know as Lent. Thus the discipline

1

of the Church was related to the great commemoration. In Canon 5 of the Council of Nicaea (AD 325), it is laid down that the first of the twice-yearly synods held to ratify sentences of excommunication must be summoned before the forty days, 'that the pure gift may be offered to God after all the bitterness has been put away'.[4] From the fourth century Lent was the occasion of public penance for those who had fallen into grievous sin. In early years, as we discover from the New Testament itself,[5] there had been doubts as to whether a second repentance was possible and much controversy about the treatment of the lapsed. After the Council of Nicaea and throughout the Middle Ages, they would be restored, after the penances of Lent, on the Thursday, or sometimes the Friday, before Easter.[6]

But the third strand is appearing. In spite of the lack of historical interest in the days when the end seemed near and Christians lived in joyful expectation of their Lord, 'the dimension of sacred memories'[7] was never wholly lacking. Justin Martyr (*c.* AD 150) refers to the 'memoirs' composed by the Apostles 'which are called Gospels'.[8] The use of the Old Testament gave to the Church a sense of even more remote history as did the carrying over into its liturgy of many of the associations of the Jewish Passover.

And it was inevitable as the centuries passed and the Church emerged from being a back-street sect into a publicly recognized body and Christianity became the official religion of the (declining) Roman Empire, that the Church would not only look back increasingly to its origins and seek to preserve its traditions in worship; it would show more awareness of times and seasons. For one thing the Church *had* more time. Though it was still believed that each returning day brought the *parousia* nearer, in effect it postponed it further into the future and gave the Church an extension of earthly time; while a company no longer proscribed and compelled to clandestine worship in moments stolen from secular duties had the luxury of as many days and hours as it wanted. There was also need and opportunity to 'spell out' to the many nominal adherents who crowded the now socially respectable churches, the meaning of the gospel, while some Christians deliberately took all the time there was for religious exercises in withdrawal from the evils of society and in the quest of entire sanctification.

Historical realism is more easily achieved in the week before Easter than at any other time. The four Gospels give a great proportion of space to the Passion Narrative. The only day-by-day account of the Lord's life is in the last week. There is enough evangelical material to govern the worship of each day and an embarrassment of riches for Thursday with the Last Supper, the institution of the Eucharist, the washing of the disciples' feet, the Johannine discourses, and the Agony in the Garden.

It seems likely, as Professor J. G. Davies has argued,[9] that Constantine's encouragement of pilgrimages to the holy places in Jerusalem fostered the keeping of Holy Week in the countries of the eastern Mediterranean. Cyril of Jerusalem's Catechetical Lectures (AD 350) seek to fix the hearts and minds of his hearers on the events of the gospel by appeal to the evidences of their surroundings – 'the palm trees in the valley ... Gethsemane ... this blessed Golgotha ... the most holy Sepulchre'.

Towards the end of the fourth century, a nun, probably named Egeria,[10] who may have come from Spain or one of the European countries with an Atlantic coast, spent three years in the Holy Land. She wrote a vivid, chatty account of the liturgical customs of Jerusalem, including the services of 'the Paschal Week', which 'they call the Great Week'. These took place in the various churches which had been erected on the sacred sites, each event being commemorated in the building dedicated to it. They were preceded by a vigil on the night of the Friday–Saturday before Palm Sunday (a title which Egeria does not use) and a commemoration of the raising of Lazarus in Bethany on the Saturday afternoon.

The procession of palms was held late on the Sunday afternoon. It was not connected with the Sunday Eucharist, but followed lengthy services of the Word in churches on the Mount of Olives. The signal for its commencement was the reading of the account of Christ's entry into Jerusalem, almost certainly from St Matthew's Gospel. The procession, which must have been slow and straggling, included old and young, 'the babies and the ones too young to walk' being 'carried on their parents' shoulders'. The bishop was the central figure, as in all the liturgical acts. The procession concluded with the usual evening office in the Anastasis or Church of the Resurrection.

Egeria particularly noted and admired the suitability of the lessons at the Jerusalem services, which suggests that she came from a church where the Bible was read in course, without regard to the appropriateness of the passage to the occasion. She also remarked on the frequency and length of the sermons.

Monday was not remarkable except for afternoon readings, suitable to the place and day, in the Martyrium or Place of Crucifixion, the church in front of the forecourt of the basilica of the Resurrection or Holy Sepulchre. As on Tuesday and Wednesday and all the other weekdays in Lent (an eight-week season in fourth-century Jerusalem) there were extra morning services. Late on Tuesday night, in the church built over the cave on the Mount of Olives in which, it was said, the Lord had taught his disciples, the bishop read the apocalyptic discourses from Matthew 21. On Wednesday night in the Anastasis the bishop read of the pact of Judas with the chief priests for the betrayal of Jesus. The people accompanied him with groans at the infamy of the deed.

The distinctive services of Thursday began at 2.00 p.m. with a Eucharist in the Martyrium at which the ministry of the Word was concentrated upon the betrayal and the death of Judas. This was followed by a second Eucharist on the theme of the Last Supper. At this latter the anaphora for the only time in the year was said 'behind the Cross'. This seems to refer to a small vestibule to the rear of the stump of rent rock which was the supposed site of Calvary.

After a hasty meal, the people then hurried to the Mount of Olives. At 7.00 p.m. the vigil commenced. Four stations were kept on the Mount of Olives, the third and fourth being in Gethsemane to commemorate the agony and the arrest. Then followed a procession, children and old people again trailing along with the rest, through the city to Calvary for the story of the trial before Pilate and finally, just before sunrise, some of the more vigorous went to Mount Sion to pray 'at the column at which the Lord was scourged'.

Good Friday proper began at 8.00 a.m. with the veneration of the relic of the cross. This lasted until noon when a three-hour service was held. This was made up of lessons and hymns, 'first from the psalms, whenever the Passion is mentioned; then from the Apostles, either from the Epistles of the Apostles or from their Acts; then the passages from the Gospels, which recount Christ's suffering'. The service ended with the reading of John 19.30 in which Jesus gives up his spirit. The three-o'clock service, usual during Holy Week, followed; then, at the Holy Sepulchre, there was read St John's account of the Lord's burial. Some of the younger and more energetic kept a further vigil through Friday night. Egeria did not go into details about Holy Saturday and Easter; she merely said that 'the paschal vigils are kept as with us', knowing that her readers would be familiar with them.

Such a glowing account was bound in time to lead to a copying of the Holy Week services in places far from Jerusalem. But, in the West, even when Holy Week was kept as a time of observance, the services of the earlier days did not attempt to follow too closely the events of the Gospels, but were concentrated on one of the Passion narratives as a whole,[11] for example Matthew on Sunday, Luke on Wednesday, John on Friday. There was no attempt to mark each day's events, though Ambrose of Milan foreshadows later developments when he says 'we must observe not only the day of the Passion but the day of the Resurrection so that we have a day of bitterness and a day of rejoicing'.

The Middle Ages saw an increasing historical emphasis with a good deal of local diversity and the addition of various ceremonies during the last three days which have become familiar to twentieth-century worshippers through Roman and Anglo-Catholic practice. There was *Tenebrae*, the twelfth-century name given to the Matins and Lauds of the triduum, the last three days of the week. It means 'darkness', since, over the centuries, these morning offices tended to be pushed back to the evening of the previous day to save people the inconvenience of rising very early. As the offices proceeded, all the lights (candles) would be extinguished save for one representing Christ, who alone shines out against the darkness of seemingly victorious evil. There was the blessing of the holy oils, that is, the oil of the catechumens, the chrism for confirmation, and the oil of the sick – this was done only by bishops in cathedrals. There was the washing of feet and the stripping of the altars, which, utilitarian in origin, came to typify the dereliction of Christ, an acting-out of Psalm 22. On Good Friday the *Reproaches* were sung before the veneration of the cross. These echo a passage in the prophet Micah, but seem to be ninth-century Gallican or Spanish in their liturgical form. Communion on Good Friday came to be given from the consecrated host of the day before, since it was felt that a celebration of the Eucharist was incompatible with the day of sorrows; hence the Mass of the Presanctified. On Holy Saturday was introduced the blessing of the new fire and the paschal candle. There was also the tendency to anticipate the ceremonies of Holy Saturday night as happened with *Tenebrae*. In 1944 the Lutheran, Dietrich Bonhoeffer, could write to a friend about Holy Week in Rome and the Easter alleluia being sung at Saturday noon.[12] The reforms of 1951 and 1955 sought to ensure that the Easter Mass did not come before midnight, though the most recent legislation modifies this to the extent of permitting a Eucharist earlier, on the Saturday evening, and regarding this as an Easter Mass, as it is if the duration of the day is reckoned from sunset to sunset as with the Jews.

The Counter-Reformation fastened the medievalism of Holy Week the more securely upon the Roman Church. It introduced the familiar non-liturgical Three Hours devotions on Good Friday based on the seven words from the cross. This originated with the Jesuits in Peru after the Lima earthquake of 1687 and has obvious affinities with the spiritual exercises of Ignatius Loyola.

The Book of Common Prayer provides an austerely scriptural commemoration, with long sections from the Old Testament and the Passion stories and a eucharistic rite which, though hardly satisfying at Christmas, Easter and Pentecost, comes into its own in Lent and Passiontide. The Alternative Service Book (1980) maintains the same principle with the fourfold eucharistic shape and a greater element of thanksgiving for the fullness of God's deed in Christ. The last quarter of a century has seen the increasing observance of Holy Week in the Church of Scotland and in the British Free Churches. There may be still some English village chapels which keep Good Friday as a day of festival – a custom which arose partly in a proper desire to assert the triumph of the gospel as against Latin gloom, partly in reaction against the devotion of the Oxford Movement. But there are now few churches which do not have special services or sing hymns such as the very ancient 'All glory, laud and honour' on Palm Sunday, and selections from the prolific eighteenth–nineteenth century hymnody of the Passion during the rest of the week. One feature of Holy Week worship in all communions in the last hundred years is the increased use of popular congregational hymns. Particularly have they had place in the Three Hours and in the less rigidly liturgical services which have been held in Nonconformist and some Anglican churches on the weekday evenings.

SOME INSIGHTS AND DEDUCTIONS

This rapid catalogue of developments helps us to distinguish certain basic principles of Holy Week observance which we are able to see perhaps in sharper focus than our fathers were, and which should govern our practice and our ecumenical partnership in the future.

1   At this season all confessions have read, dramatized and expounded more Scripture than at any other – the Gospel narratives of the Passion, the apostolic interpretations, and the prefigurement in 'Moses, the prophets and the psalms'. The 'things concerning Jesus' are thus placed in a wide context of sacred history. Mount Moriah, the Red Sea, the crossing of Jordan, the Babylonian captivity and the anguish of patriarchs, prophets and unnamed psalmists are all in some sense 'stations'

7

of the cross. The Jews believed that the Temple at Jerusalem stood on the site of Abraham's sacrifice of Isaac; while medieval Christians imagined that Calvary was also the place of Adam's fall and created legends of the wood of the cross being taken from a tree planted on Adam's grave, from which also had come the twig which the dove brought to Noah in the ark to tell him that the destroying flood was past.

Nor are these analogies and types confined to the traditions of the Bible. In *The Paschal Mystery* Louis Bouyer sees in the pagan mysteries 'a rough draft, very pale and inadequate, of what God is preparing to give man in answer to his deepest desires and infinitely in excess of his most sanguine hopes'.[13] It has also been urged that instead of being disturbed or embarrassed by the widespread oriental myth of the dying and rising God, Christians should find in it 'positive value', for it is Jesus who fulfils the ancient patterns of those far-off ritual re-enactments and did in reality what the myth foreshadows. Other Christian thinkers have heard the reverberations of the deed which shook the earth and blotted out the sun far beyond the ancient world and its myths. F. W. Dillistone in *The Novelists and the Passion Story* and Professors MacKinnon and Tinsley, in various writings, have shown how the study of human relationships in great literature demands the concept of atonement.[14]

The Holy Week commemoration, therefore, will take the tradition of the sufferings, death and resurrection of Jesus and relate it to the whole of human history, the aspirations of other faiths and cultures and the travail of the created universe. In consequence, the devotion will not be concentrated entirely upon the details and instruments of the Passion which the New Testament describes with brevity and restraint, or be a perpetual return to Golgotha 'to watch the sacred blood drip to the ground'. The 'things concerning Jesus' will reveal, as in a sudden lightning flash, the truth about our existence from first creation to the end of the age.

Of course, the Christian who feels that the categories of Scripture still have meaning for our age will want to express this more dynamically than the Christian who would prefer to substitute 'ultimate reality' for 'God', or 'the Christ-event' for 'the acts of God in Christ'. One of the most ancient interpretations of the Passion is found in Peter's Pentecost sermon in the Acts of the Apostles:

> When he had been given up to you by the deliberate will and plan of God, you used heathen men to crucify and kill him. But God raised him to life again, setting him free from the pangs of death, because it could not be that death should keep him in its grip. God has made this Jesus, whom you crucified, both Lord and Messiah.[15]

But whatever mode of interpretation is congenial to us, whether we take this language *au pied de la lettre* or regard it as the poetic account of a corporate experience too deep for words, our Holy Week services must declare deliverance from frustration and mortality for all men and all creatures and foreshadow the liberty and splendour of the children of God.

2 In Holy Week we are concerned with history. One of the crucial differences between the Christian mystery and all others, between the Christian story and some profound work of fiction is that it is largely open to historical criticism. It is not possible to reconstruct with certainty the events of the last week of our Lord's life; the Gospels differ as to the order and the timing, while the trial narratives are notoriously confused. But that Jesus lived, behaved in the ways attributed to him and provoked simultaneously adoring love and virulent opposition, was much misunderstood by his friends and his enemies, knew overwhelming mental and spiritual stress and conflict and was arrested, tried, condemned and put to death by the brutal Roman penalty of crucifixion, is beyond dispute. So also is the fact that his followers were convinced that God had 'raised him from the dead'. Christian worship is the remembering of Jesus and what happened to him and what the early Christians believed about him, as facts of history.

Anamnesis, the word used in St Paul's account of the institution of the Eucharist, which he claimed was 'received from the Lord' – 'Do this in *remembrance* of me' – has been the subject of much rigorous examination and sophisticated speculation.[16] It has become almost a platitude to assert that it must not be 'impoverished to mean only a pious recollection which remains irretrievably beyond recall' though, inevitably, this is being questioned.[17]

There is really no need to go beyond what 'remembering' means in profounder human experience to outlaw reductionism once and for all. John Donne declared in a sermon: '*Plato* plac'd *all learning* in the memory; wee may place *all Religion* in the memory too. All knowledge, that seems new today, says *Plato*, is but a remembring of that, which your soul knew before. All instruction which we can give you today, is but the remembring free of the mercies of God, which have been *new every morning.*' The late E. M. Forster, the renowned humanist man of letters, pointed out that the title of Marcel Proust's novel, which he regarded as second only to Tolstoy's *War and Peace*, was not 'Things Past' but 'Remembrance of Things Past'. 'What really matters in the book is not the events but the remembering of events.' No one dare say that, in Christian worship, the events are secondary to the recall, and yet, like poetry, according to Aristotle, worship may be truer than history in so far as memory enables us to see past events from differing perspectives. To quote Forster on Proust again: 'It reconsiders the same episode, the same characters, and reaches new results. It keeps turning the stuff of life about and looking through it from this direction and that.'[18] (This is one reason why preaching and meditation are so essential a part of worship.)

But it is the paschal background of the Last Supper, which is indisputable, whether we regard it as actually a Passover meal or not, which guides us to a fuller and more exact interpretation of *anamnesis*. In the Passover, as Professor Reid has pointed out so very clearly, 'the transmitter of the tradition explicitly identifies himself with those who were contemporary with the original Exodus–Passover events'. Dr Reid quotes Theo Preiss: 'Each time he celebrated [the annual Passover], according to the famous rabbinical dictum [the Jew] was expected to think of himself as leaving Egypt.'[19] The Jewish father says '*we* were Pharaoh's bondmen in Egypt; and the Lord brought *us* out of Egypt' and gives as the reason for the Passover 'that which the Lord did unto *me* when *I* came forth out of Egypt'. Thus in the act of remembrance the past is made present.

Some of Wesley's *Hymns on the Lord's Supper* show a like understanding in the case of the Eucharist:

> Endless scenes of wonder rise
> From that mysterious tree,
> Crucified before our eyes
> Where we our Maker see.
>
> O that our faith may never move,
> But stand unshaken as thy love!
> Sure evidence of things unseen,
> Now let it pass the years between
> And view thee bleeding on the tree
> My God, who dies for me, for me.[20]

But this is not all. In the Passover this remembrance is also 'loosed from the limitations that time ordinarily imposes between past and future'.[21] There is the verse of the second Hallel Psalm, 'Blessed be he that cometh in the name of the Lord'.[22]

> The Mishnaic exposition of the Passover includes a reference to the four cups in the rite, and these are related symbolically to the four cups of punishment which appear in Jer. xxv. 15, li 7; Pss. lxxv 9, xi 6 – cups which manifestly belong to future time. Hence Strack-Billerbeck can draw the conclusion (*ad* Luke xxii 19) that, while the Passover is of course a *Gedàchtnisfeier* including thanks for redemption in the past, it was also directed towards the future and a final redemption to come.[23]

This also applies to the Christian *anamnesis* and to the worship of Holy Week. The history of Jesus and all that it means in its eternal consequences is appropriated by the worshippers. They remember him and it is as though they were present all the way from his cradle to his cross – and beyond. But also they grasp in advance the future kingdom, the new life in the new world of which the early Christians were so conscious.

It is a frequent and not ill-deserved criticism that the Church lives too much in the past, and it is particularly serious in an age when the changes of a millennium have been crowded into half a century and the minds of our contemporaries are directed to the future, not only in secular (and sometimes apocalyptic) hope, but also in secular despair. The eschatological futuristic notes of baptism and the Eucharist should be sounded loud and clear in Holy Week: 'Behold, I make all things new.'[24]

3   The mood of Holy Week should not therefore be predominantly of mourning. The loud sighs and groans at the indignities Christ suffered, which Egeria describes as being audible from the Mount of Olives to the city of Jerusalem, must not drown the alleluias which the Eastern Orthodox Churches do not silence, even in Lent. In the West, Holy Week has been too heavy with sorrow, with that pity for Jesus in his sufferings, which he himself discouraged, and there has been over it at times a pall of morbidity and gloom. Yet Christian cheerfulness is not easy; the hope of God's final triumph has to be held amid the groaning and travail of the whole creation and part of the secret of the appeal of the cross has been in its identification of Christ with humanity in its greatest wretchedness and need. The crucifixion was, in the terms of this world, a murder and defeat, which corresponds all too closely to what we see around us. 'Truth for ever on the scaffold, wrong for ever on the throne.' Perhaps the only way to bear the unspeakable horrors of Calvary (or Auschwitz), to contemplate them and still maintain our hope in a world in which such atrocities are possible, is somehow to come to terms with them liturgically.[25] But this demands a liturgy and spirit of worship far removed from casual, light-hearted churchgoing. The joy is the other side of bitter pain and our observance cannot shirk the fact. Perhaps the truth is found in the Archbishop's sermon in T. S. Eliot's *Murder in the Cathedral*: 'It is only in these our Christian mysteries that we can rejoice and mourn at once for the same reason.'[26]

4   More than our feelings are involved as we participate in the drama of Holy Week. We commemorate acts with which

we are to be identified not only in our emotions but in our lives. This brings us again to the significance of baptism, which the early Church included in the Easter vigil and which, according to St Paul, is a dying and being buried and rising again with Christ. It is still good, where possible, to include baptism in the Saturday ceremonies. And either then, or, at some other time during the week, there should be a renewal of baptismal vows. This, with its emphasis on the difference Christ makes to our entire selves, also, as we have already implied, adds to the eschatological notes of Holy Week worship. 'It does not yet appear what we shall be.'

5   The manifold ceremonies and liturgical practices, which have grown up, proclaim the Word by many means in addition to hearing. There is sight, Bunyan's 'eye-gate'; there is movement, in, for example, the Palm Sunday procession or the Good Friday veneration of Christ crucified; and there is the participation of the people in these and many ways, some conventional, like hymn-singing and responsive litanies, others less so, like dramatic readings from the Gospels, or the feet-washing. Free-Church and Protestant worship, which it is now generally recognized has been too much confined to 'ear-gate', can benefit especially by the introduction at this season of some of the ancient rites.

THE SERVICES

If there is one conclusion which cries aloud from what we have outlined, it is that the service which should dominate the Holy Week, as all the Christian year, is the Eucharist. This, as the early Christians realized, is the act which encapsulates the whole of our redemption and the more intensely historical observance of Holy Week is but a prolonged meditation of what is contained in every Eucharist. That is why all the services which follow have been given a eucharistic shape, that is, they are in two principal parts, the Ministry of the Word and the Ministry of the Sacrament; and also why each one of the first series seeks to accentuate some aspect of the Eucharist, for example penitence. It is recognized that whether or not the services always culminate in the Lord's Supper will depend on church tradition as well as on a variety of local considerations. What must never be forgotten is the Reformed custom of what is somewhat technically called 'the dry anaphora' (that is, prayer of oblation without the sacramental species of bread or wine). This is always thanksgiving, Eucharist, which John Knox, for instance, saw as the primary meaning of the Supper. Christ's death was 'shown forth' that 'ye shall laud, magnify and extol the liberal kindness of God the Father and the infinite benefits which ye have received by Christ's death'.[27] On Palm Sunday, Maundy Thursday and, above all, on Easter Day, the Supper would seem to be the natural climax. Good Friday is disputable and strong arguments for and against a celebration may be advanced. These are rehearsed below.

(A) PRINCIPAL SERVICES

Palm Sunday to Wednesday

On Palm Sunday we have provided for a procession. This and not the distribution of the palms is the principal ceremony preceding divine service. The Eucharist, or main service in church to which the procession is intended to lead, will, of course, take the form customary in the particular parish or congregation. The Matthaean or Marcan Passion narratives may be read and there are arrangements for these to be dramatized for three voices and possibly a chorus.

For Monday, Tuesday and Wednesday there are two sets of services. The former are based on the themes of Penitence, Obedience and Service respectively. The Tuesday order, 'Obedience', draws heavily on the Methodist Covenant Service and is, in effect, a renewal of baptismal vows which, in a more traditional form, is part of the liturgy of Saturday/Sunday. The duplication is deliberate. The Tuesday service may be used to give opportunity to those who may not be able to be present on Saturday.

The second series of services makes possible a historical commemoration following the accounts of the Synoptic Gospels. Monday is the Day of Cleansing, Tuesday of Teaching, Wednesday of Waiting. This last includes the betrayal – 'Spy Wednesday' is an old English name for it – but our title focuses on the Lord, not the traitor.

Maundy Thursday

The Church on this day gathers as if in the Upper Room. The Collects commemorate the institution of the Eucharist and in alternate years either the Pauline account from 1 Corinthians 11 or the Marcan narrative are read. A feature of the service is to follow a Reformed tradition which uses at every Eucharist the former passage as a 'warrant' or narrative of the institution read before the elements are taken. This is also a Roman Catholic custom on Maundy Thursday.

The Gospel of the feet-washing is prescribed for the first year and as it is read the washing itself may take place; or it may be postponed to a later point in the service to accompany select verses from John 13. It is often the case for a group of twelve from the congregation to be washed; but sometimes, if the number is not too large, for the whole company. It may be done just before communion; or even outside the liturgy at an *agape* meal in advance.

At the end of the service there may be a 'stripping of the altars', that is, a removal of even the austere Lenten array and ornaments from the church if it be of 'Catholic' practice, and/or a form of *Tenebrae* (see page 117). If this custom is followed, the departure of the people from a darkened church may well be in some disorder, without musical accompaniment and somewhat stumbling, to simulate the bewilderment, fear and desertion of the disciples at the arrest of Jesus.

In some churches, what remains of the Eucharist will be borne to a side chapel and laid on an 'altar of repose'. A vigil may be kept, throughout the night or for some hours.

Good Friday

The crucial and controversial question is 'Eucharist or no?' The Western tradition has been for this, with the Saturday following, to be an aliturgical day. As the one sacrifice takes place on the cross, we do not seek to commemorate it in its sacramental form but to remain in wonder and worship before the event in history itself. The Roman Catholic Church is not likely to depart from this practice. But then there arises the matter of communion. The 'Mass of the Pre-Sanctified' was intended to be the means whereby the sacrament might be received from the reserved host, consecrated on Maundy Thursday. Although the title has now been dropped, the practice still persists in Roman Catholic and High Anglican churches.

In the Roman Church on the Continent, communion on Good Friday is ceasing to be the custom. The Church's worship then and on Saturday is seen as an extended ministry of the Word, the spoken (and silent) proclamation of the death of the incarnate Lord. This finds its completion in the Resurrection Eucharist of Easter, so that the whole liturgy from Good Friday to Easter Morning may be seen as a solemn and glorious unity of Word and Sacrament.

There is, however, an alternative view, which may be increasing its hold in the Church of England. This would maintain that the day from which flow all the life and ordinances of the Christian faith is supremely appropriate for the Eucharist. This is the day when above all we should give thanks for our redemption through the Lord's appointed means. The remembrance of Calvary is more suitably achieved through the Eucharist as a whole than by a total preoccupation with the historic events, and since, for us, 'every Good Friday is *after* Easter', a true theology must set the Passion in its full context.

We have allowed for both views. There may or may not be a eucharistic celebration according to conviction or custom. But we have included the ancient rite, described by Egeria, of the veneration of the cross, with the Reproaches and the late-sixth-century hymn of Venantius Fortunatus, Bishop of Poitiers, *'Pange lingua'*, 'Sing my tongue the glorious battle'. Ten verses are printed, but this is to allow for those congregations where each individual will venerate the cross. Where the ceremony is corporate, a selection of verses may be sung.

The Easter Vigil

The Vigil begins with five lessons read by the light of the lectern lamp in a darkened church. The first is from the story of the creation in Genesis 1, the next two are of the plight of God's people in Egypt and subsequent deliverance, the fourth is St Paul's teaching on baptism as our dying and rising with Christ, and the fifth is the record of the appearance of the risen Lord in St Matthew.

Then follows the Service of Light, with the Paschal candle from which the other candles in the church are lit to symbolize the spreading of the gospel throughout the world by the witness of Christians. This is succeeded by the great Easter proclamation, the *Exultet*, and then possibly by a sermon, and the Sacrament of Holy Baptism should any candidates be available. Then the whole congregation renews its baptismal vows according to the appropriate rite of the church in which the service is held and the service may culminate in the Eucharist.

Despite Dom Gregory Dix's suggestion that the pre-Nicene corporate vigils of the Church are an 'invention of manuals of liturgical history',[28] there was always among Christians a tendency to come together to await the Lord's return. The hours of darkness were particularly suggestive of the return because of the references in the Gospels to the Lord coming as a thief in the night, or the bridegroom appearing at midnight.

Whether or not the Easter Vigil was a development of a weekly practice, there is no doubt that it was firmly established in the pre-Nicene Church and, as we noted at the beginning of this essay, was the principal celebration of what was not merely the feast *par excellence*, but the only feast beside which no other could exist. It was an essential part of the 'celebration of the resurrection and a present partaking of Christ's victory through death and rising to life again; it was a joyful feast of the deliverance of believers through faith in Christ and baptism in his name'.[29] It ought to continue to hold a special place in the calendar of the Church because it alone preserves the primitive Christian emphasis and practice.[30]

This form of service obviously has its roots in the Western order, but it seeks to proclaim the totality of the redemption wrought in Christ and uses the Service of Light as a symbol of the climax of what God has done through him. The key to the understanding of the whole service is not in the fact of our entrance into the Church but of Christ's entrance into the world. Therefore the readings have been placed first; they relate those events which the Service of Light presupposes – the creation, the deliverance from Egypt and the passion and resurrection of the Lord – and are chosen on the principle that a clear unity must be seen to exist between light, baptism and Eucharist.

The relation of the Eucharist in which the Saturday evening service finds its climax to the celebrations of the next day constitutes a problem. As we have noted, the latest Roman Catholic ruling is that, even if held before midnight, this is the Easter Eucharist. Some, in spite of ancient precedent, will feel that this is psychologically wrong. The women went to the sepulchre at early dawn and there is something of peculiar atmosphere and devotional power about Easter morning.[31] Three other possibilities may be indicated. The whole rite with communion could be held on Easter Eve, *concluding after midnight*; the whole rite with communion could take place very early on Easter Day; the rite on Easter Eve could end after the baptismal reaffirmation or with the Milner-White *Litany of Resurrection* and the people could return to church for communion on Easter Day.

A case may be made out for two Easter Eucharists, differently regarded. The Saturday Eucharist – in the evening or at midnight – is the Paschal mystery, the commemoration of the deliverance of God, which was indeed wrought in darkness, hidden from the sight of human eyes. The Sunday communion celebrates the glorious reunion of the Lord with his disciples, when he speaks to them by name and gives his peace and commissions them in the power of the Holy Spirit. 'He was known in the breaking of the bread.'

We have not provided for every single ceremony of Holy Week worship and we realize that some churches will want to add customs which to other traditions might feel strange.[32] The Maundy Thursday service, for instance, may be thought of as being, in our fashionable jargon, 'open-ended'. It could be followed by the stripping of the altars with or without a *Tenebrae*-like ceremony of the extinction of lights, and/or a watch in commemoration of Gethsemane. These themselves may be carried out with varying degrees of elaboration. Psalm 22 may be read in the course of the stripping; or if this is felt to be uniquely for Good Friday, Psalm 88; or it may be done, as now with the Roman Church, in silence. The watch may last no more than an hour, or, as with the Roman Church, continue until midnight but not after, or be maintained until dawn. The proximity of the Easter Vigil may influence the decision.

Before the Easter Vigil, there may be a blessing of the new fire, from which the Paschal candle may be lit. This probably has its origins in heathen custom, but has been given Christian reference for many centuries. It is mentioned in accounts of pilgrimages to Jerusalem as early as 870. The lighting of the candles during the Vigil was deemed to be miraculous, though a Muslim visitor in 926 ascribes it to 'a clever artifice'. The flame was probably brought furtively from the lamp which burned before the sepulchre, which would account for the complained-of uncertainty and variability of the time of its appearance.[33]

Today the fire may be prepared and kindled outside the church or, as John Martin has written, 'reliably and expeditiously obtained from one of the heavier types of cigarette lighter'.[34] A prayer with scriptural references to fire of glory, of judgement and of cleansing may be appropriate.

The ceremonies which accompany the marking of the candle may be used. Again we quote John Martin:

The Easter Candle is a large and heavy column of wax, for it must burn all this night and at service time from today until the Eucharist of Ascensiontide, when it is extinguished after the reading of the Gospel. Thus it is conceived of as a symbol of the Risen Christ, and this is made clear by the ceremonies which immediately precede its lighting and blessing. First it is marked with the sign of the Cross, the Greek letters A and O, and the figures of the current year of redemption, while the celebrant says, 'Christ, yesterday and today, the beginning and the end, Alpha and Omega; his are all times and ages; to him be the glory and dominion, for ever and ever. Amen'. Then five studs (in the Roman rite five grains of incense) representing the wounds which the Risen Body of Christ still bore, are inserted into the wax of the candle, with the words, 'By his holy and glorious wounds may Christ our Lord guard and preserve us. Amen'. The candle is lighted from the new fire to the accompaniment of a single prayer for the lightening of our darkness, and blessed with a formula ... which links the thought of our walking as children of light (Eph. 5.8) with prayer for a fruitful partaking of the Holy Communion.[35]

These additional ceremonies are not essential to Holy Week, but are precious and valuable to large numbers of Christians, and we would not discourage them. Our last wish is to impose a rigid uniformity. The basic observances demand nothing more than a congregation with water, bread and wine, and the Holy Scriptures. The point at which the elaboration of these ceases to be an enrichment and turns to confusion will differ with differing temperaments and traditions, though there are some of us to whom God is eager to come in ways other than those of our own fathers, and to reveal himself in forms we had thought were alien.

(B)   THE DAILY OFFICE AND PSALMS

It is assumed that the principal services will be supported by the daily offices either said corporately or in private. *The Daily Office Revised* (SPCK 1978) incorporates the lessons and psalms of the first edition of this manual (1971).

In the effort to be realistic we have prescribed for the daily office but one psalm for the morning and one for the evening and thus have avoided duplication. The Psalter is always central to the office and never more so than in Holy Week. The gospel tradition says that Psalms 22.1 and 31.5 were on our Lord's lips in death, and, according to St Luke, Jesus taught his disciples that the Psalms, as well as the Law and the Prophets, foretold his sufferings and victory.[36] The Psalms of enthronement and ascent as well as the cries of penitence and complaint all seem to prefigure the drama of the Passion.

We are aware that the modern Easter is the first weekend holiday of the year and that, in any case, it is almost impossible to expect more than comparatively few people to share with the Church in all of its services from Palm Sunday to Easter Day. Any hope of the majority even of committed church members attending a complete Holy Week course seems unrealistic, though there are heartening signs of increased numbers. We have therefore felt it expedient as well as principled to keep in mind the primitive unity in every service and to set forth the whole of our redemption on each occasion, though attention will be focused on different aspects and incidents.

Recent years have seen a revival of charismatic evangelicalism which has its vogue among all age-groups as well as in some of the Black churches of the inner cities. What we offer here may not be altogether in tune with its enthusiasm, which tends to be less ordered though no less ritualistic, and sometimes lacking in the richness of historical memory and in the tragic dimension of the gospel. But there is evidence that men and women are hungering for a way of life and worship which confronts the total realities and mystery of the universe. This the keeping of Holy Week enables them to do, provided that it is not an escape into the sanctuary from discomfort and disturbance, and that we do not turn the words of Christ in his utter Passion into liturgical formulae. Let our serious contemporaries see that the Church has a faith to proclaim which plumbs the very depths of human experience, and that worship is not an antiquated pastime but the appropriation of a love which gives – and takes – everything; and some at least will gladly seek to know Christ in the fellowship of his sufferings and the power of his resurrection and to take part with the Church in the celebration of those acts which are greater than the making of the world.

NOTES

1   Cf. Oliver C. Quick, *The Gospel of the New World* (Nisbet 1944), p. 88, who argues that whereas Cranmer's liturgy invites those who intend to lead 'a' new life, St Paul or St John would have surely written 'the'.

2   Epistle to Barnabas, 15.

3   F. E. Brightman, 'The Quartodeciman Question' in *JTS*, xxv (1924), p. 268.

4   See A. Allan McArthur, *The Evolution of the Christian Year* (SCM 1953), p. 115 and the whole book on the whole subject.

5   E.g., Hebrews 10.26. Cf. W. Telfer, *The Forgiveness of Sins* (SCM 1959).

6   See J. G. Davies, *Holy Week: A Short History* (Lutterworth Press 1963), pp. 47–8.

7   Georges Florovsky, 'The Worshipping Church' in *The Festal Menaion*; Eng. trans., Mother Mary and Archimandrite Kallistos Ware (Faber 1969), p. 27.

8   Justin, *Apology* 1.66.

9   Op. cit., chapter ii.

10 For these paragraphs I am especially indebted to John Wilkinson, *Egeria's Travels* (SPCK 1971) and also to Davies and McArthur, op. cit.

11 This has always been so in the Roman Mass, from which at this point the Book of Common Prayer does not depart. The Alternative Service Book (1980) maintains the principle with transpositions of readings and a two-year cycle.

12 D. Bonhoeffer, *Letters and Papers from Prison* (SCM 1967), p. 134.

13 L. Bouyer, *The Paschal Mystery*, p. xix.

14 Cf. John Sturdy, 'Jesus, Tammuz and the Deuteronomist' in *Church Quarterly*, vol. 2, no. 14, pp. 330ff; F. W. Dillistone, op. cit. (Collins 1960); D. M. MacKinnon, *Borderlands of Theology*

(Lutterworth 1968), pp. 97ff; 'Subjective and Objective Conceptions of Atonement' in *Prospect for Theology*, ed. F. G. Healey (Nisbet 1966), pp. 167ff, in William Purcell (ed.), *The Resurrection* (Mowbrays 1966), *passim*, and *The Problem of Metaphysics* (CUP 1974), *passim*. E. J. Tinsley's relevant lectures and broadcasts have not yet been published, except for a piece in *Theology*, 1982, pp. 98ff.

15 Acts 2.23, 24, 36.

16 E.g., Gregory Dix, *The Shape of the Liturgy* (Dacre Press 1945); D. R. Jones, *JTS* n.s. 6, lxx (1955); Joachim Jeremias, *The Eucharistic Words of Jesus* (SCM 1966).

17 John K. S. Reid, 'In Remembrance of Me' in *Church Service Society Annual*, May 1960, pp. 16–17. Contrast R. T. Beckwith, *The Study of Liturgy* (ed. Jones, Yarnold and Wainwright) (SPCK 1978), p. 49, where this is the categorical, undefended statement: 'The claim that *anamnesis* and its equivalents in the Passover denote the making present or effective of a past event is without linguistic or Jewish support.'

18 John Donne, *Sermons* (ed.) George R. Potter and Evelyn M. Simpson (Berkeley and Los Angeles 1953–62), ii. 74.
E. M. Forster, *Two Cheers for Democracy* (Penguin Books 1965), p. 228.
Cf. Samuel Johnson, 'It is not sufficiently considered, that men more frequently require to be reminded than informed' (*The Rambler*, no. 2).

19 Op. cit., pp. 9, 10. The reference is to T. Preiss, *Life in Christ* (SCM 1954), p. 20.

20 John and Charles Wesley, *Hymns on the Lord's Supper*, 21,5.

21 J. K. S. Reid, op. cit., p. 8.

22 Psalm 118.26.

23 Reid, ibid., p. 8.

24 Revelation 21.5.

25 Cf. U. E. Simon, *A Theology of Auschwitz* (1967, SPCK 1980), p. 47.

26 T. S. Eliot, *Murder in the Cathedral* (Faber 1946 edn), p. 48.

27 Quoted by Lord Eustace Percy, *John Knox* (1964 edn James Clarke), p. 117.

28 Gregory Dix, *The Shape of the Liturgy*, p. 325.

29 C. P. M. Jones (ed.), *A Manual for Holy Week* (SPCK 1967), p. 7.

30 Cf. C. Howell, *Preparing for Easter* (Burns & Oates edn), p. 7.

31   See G. B. Timms, 'Anglican Adaptations of the Roman Rite' in C. P. M. Jones, op. cit., pp. 72ff.

32   For valuable guidance see John T. Martin, *Christ our Passover* (SCM 1958) and the various editions of the new Roman Holy Week Book (Geoffrey Chapman 1971), and C. P. M. Jones, op. cit.

33   See Gabriel Bertonière, *The Historical Development of the Easter Vigil and Related Services in the Greek Church*, Orientalia Christiana Analecta (Rome 1972), pp. 40ff.

34   John T. Martin, op. cit., p. 41.

35   Ibid., pp. 41–2.

36   Luke 24.44.

PALM SUNDAY

The Triumphant Entry

The commemoration of our Lord's triumphant entry into
Jerusalem immediately precedes the main service of Palm
Sunday.
If there is to be a procession, the service may begin in some
place other than the church.
Palms may be distributed before the service begins or after the
prayer (section 4).

1 SENTENCE

> Hosanna to the Son of David! Blessed is he who comes in
> the name of the Lord!
> Hosanna in the highest!

2 INTRODUCTION

The service may be introduced with these or other similar
words.

> We come together to begin this week in which we
> celebrate Christ's death and resurrection. Let us
> remember the entry of Christ in triumph into his own
> city and follow him with a lively faith.

3 GOSPEL

Matthew 21.1–11

When they drew near to Jerusalem and came to Bethphage, to
the Mount of Olives, then Jesus sent two disciples, saying to them,
'Go into the village opposite you, and immediately you
will find an ass tied, and a colt with her; untie them and bring
them to me. If any one says anything to you, you shall say,
"The Lord has need of them", and he will send them
immediately.' This took place to fulfil what was spoken by the
prophet, saying,

'Tell the daughter of Zion,
Behold, your king is coming to you,
humble, and mounted on an ass,
and on a colt, the foal of an ass.'

The disciples went and did as Jesus had directed them; they
brought the ass and the colt, and put their garments on them,
and he sat thereon. Most of the crowd spread their garments
on the road, and others cut branches from the trees and spread
them on the road. And the crowds that went before him
shouted, 'Hosanna to the Son of David! Blessed be he who
comes in the name of the Lord! Hosanna in the highest!' And
when he entered Jerusalem, all the city was stirred, saying,
'Who is this?' And the crowds said, 'This is the prophet Jesus
from Nazareth of Galilee.'

or *Mark 11.1–11*

When they drew near to Jerusalem, to Bethphage and
Bethany, at the Mount of Olives, he sent two of his disciples,
and said to them, 'Go into the village opposite you, and
immediately as you enter it you will find a colt tied, on which
no one has ever sat; untie it and bring it. If any one says to
you, "Why are you doing this?" say, "The Lord has need of it
and will send it back here immediately." ' And they went away,
and found a colt tied at the door out in the open street; and
they untied it. And those who stood there said to them, 'What
are you doing, untying the colt?' And they told them what
Jesus had said; and they let them go. And they brought the
colt to Jesus, and threw their garments on it; and he sat upon
it. And many spread their garments on the road, and others
spread leafy branches which they had cut from the fields. And
those who went before and those who followed cried out,
'Hosanna! Blessed be he who comes in the name of the Lord!
Blessed be the kingdom of our father David that is coming!
Hosanna in the highest!' And he entered Jerusalem, and went
into the temple; and when he had looked round at everything,
as it was already late, he went out to Bethany with the twelve.

4   PRAYER

> Lord, increase the faith of your people
> and listen to our prayers:
> Today we honour Christ our King by commemorating
>   his entry into Jerusalem.
> May we honour you every day by living always in him,
> who is alive and reigns for ever and ever. **Amen.**

or

> Almighty God,
> whose Son Jesus Christ was greeted on this day as King:
> Help us now to honour him by carrying these
>   branches of palm,
> and always to seek your glory by obedience to your will;
> through Jesus Christ our Lord. **Amen.**

5   SENTENCE

> The people of the Hebrews carrying palms and olive
> branches went to meet the Lord, shouting, 'Hosanna in
> the highest!'

6   HYMN, during which all may carry palms and may go *in
    procession* either from some other place to the church or within
    the church.

> *All glory, laud and honour*
> *To thee, Redeemer, King,*
> *To whom the lips of children*
> *Made sweet hosannas ring!*
>
> Thou art the King of Israel,
> Thou David's royal son,
> Who in the Lord's name comest,
> The King and blessed one.
> *All glory, laud and honour etc.*

27

> The company of angels
> Are praising thee on high,
> And mortal men and all things
> Created make reply.
> *All glory, laud and honour etc.*
>
> The people of the Hebrews
> With palms before thee went;
> Our praise, and prayer, and anthems
> Before thee we present.
> *All glory, laud and honour etc.*
>
> To thee before thy passion
> They sang their hymns of praise;
> To thee now high exalted
> Our melody we raise.
> *All glory, laud and honour etc.*
>
> Thou didst accept their praises;
> Accept the prayers we bring,
> Who in all good delightest,
> Thou good and gracious King.
> *All glory, laud and honour etc.*

Other hymns and psalms may also be sung, such as Psalm 24.

7   SENTENCE

> The people of the Hebrews spread their garments on the
> road and shouted, 'Hosanna to the Son of David! Blessed
> is he who comes in the name of the Lord!'

The Main Service

8   The main service of the day follows, commemorating especially
the passion of our Lord, beginning with the Collect.

COLLECT

> Almighty and everlasting God,
> who in your tender love towards mankind
>   sent your son our Saviour Jesus Christ
> to take upon him our flesh
> and to suffer death upon the cross:
> grant that we may follow the example
>   of his patience and humility,
> and also be made partakers of his resurrection;
> through Jesus Christ our Lord. **Amen.**

or

> Almighty God,
> whose most dear Son went not up to joy
>   but first he suffered pain,
> and entered not into glory before he was crucified:
> mercifully grant that we, walking in the way of the cross,
> may find it none other than the way of life and peace;
> through Jesus Christ your Son our Lord,
> who is alive and reigns with you and the Holy Spirit,
> one God, for ever and ever. **Amen.**

9   READINGS

Old Testament

Zechariah 9.9–12

> Rejoice greatly, O daughter of Zion!
>   Shout aloud, O daughter of Jerusalem!
> Lo, your king comes to you;
>   triumphant and victorious is he,
> humble and riding on an ass,
>   on a colt the foal of an ass.
> I will cut off the chariot from Ephraim
>   and the war horse from Jerusalem;
> and the battle bow shall be cut off,
>   and he shall command peace to the nations;

his dominion shall be from sea to sea,
  and from the River to the ends of the earth.
As for you also, because of the blood of my covenant with you,
  I will set your captives free from the waterless pit.
Return to your stronghold, O prisoners of hope;
  today I declare that I will restore to you double.

or *Isaiah 52.13—53 end*

Behold, my servant shall prosper,
  he shall be exalted and lifted up,
  and shall be very high.
As many were astonished at him –
  his appearance was so marred, beyond human semblance,
  and his form beyond that of the sons of men –
so shall he startle many nations;
  kings shall shut their mouths because of him;
for that which has not been told them they shall see,
  and that which they have not heard they shall understand.

Who has believed what we have heard?
  And to whom has the arm of the Lord been revealed?
For he grew up before him like a young plant,
  and like a root out of dry ground;
he had no form or comeliness that we should look at him,
  and no beauty that we should desire him.
He was despised and rejected by men;
  a man of sorrows, and acquainted with grief,
and as one from whom men hide their faces
  he was despised, and we esteemed him not.

Surely he has borne our griefs
  and carried our sorrows;
yet we esteemed him stricken,
  smitten by God, and afflicted.
But he was wounded for our transgressions,
  he was bruised for our iniquities;
upon him was the chastisement that made us whole,
  and with his stripes we are healed.

All we like sheep have gone astray;
  we have turned every one to his own way;
and the Lord has laid on him
  the iniquity of us all.

He was oppressed, and he was afflicted,
  yet he opened not his mouth;
like a lamb that is led to the slaughter,
  and like a sheep that before its shearers is dumb,
  so he opened not his mouth.
By oppression and judgment he was taken away;
  and as for his generation, who considered
that he was cut off out of the land of the living,
  stricken for the transgression of my people?
And they made his grave with the wicked
  and with a rich man in his death,
although he had done no violence,
  and there was no deceit in his mouth.

Yet it was the will of the Lord to bruise him;
  he has put him to grief;
when he makes himself an offering for sin,
  he shall see his offspring, he shall prolong his days;
the will of the Lord shall prosper in his hand;
  he shall see the fruit of the travail of his soul
    and be satisfied;
by his knowledge shall the righteous one, my servant,
  make many to be accounted righteous;
  and he shall bear their iniquities.
Therefore I will divide him a portion with the great,
  and he shall divide the spoil with the strong;
because he poured out his soul to death,
  and was numbered with the transgressors;
yet he bore the sin of many,
  and made intercession for the transgressors.

10 One of the following psalms, or a hymn.

Psalm 22.1–11

1   My God, my God, why have you forsaken me:
    why are you so far from helping me
        and from the words of my groaning?

2   My God, I cry to you by day, but you do not answer:
    and by night also I take no rest.

3   But you continue holy:
    you that are the praise of Israel.

4   In you our fathers trusted:
    they trusted, and you delivered them;

5   To you they cried and they were saved:
    they put their trust in you and were not confounded.

6   But as for me, I am a worm and no man:
    the scorn of men and despised by the people.

7   All those that see me laugh me to scorn:
    they shoot out their lips at me and wag their heads,
        saying,

8   'He trusted in the Lord – let him deliver him:
    let him deliver him, if he delights in him.'

9   But you are he that took me out of the womb:
    that brought me to lie at peace on my mother's breast.

10 On you have I been cast since my birth:
    you are my God, even from my mother's womb.

11 O go not from me, for trouble is hard at hand:
    and there is none to help.

or *Psalm 24*

1   The earth is the Lord's and all that is in it:
    the compass of the world and those who dwell therein.

2   For he has founded it upon the seas:
     and established it upon the waters.

3   Who shall ascend the hill of the Lord:
     or who shall stand in his holy place?

4   He that has clean hands and a pure heart:
     who has not set his soul upon idols,
          nor sworn his oath to a lie.

5   He shall receive blessing from the Lord:
     and recompense from the God of his salvation.

6   Of such a kind as this are those who seek him:
     those who seek your face, O God of Jacob.

7   Lift up your heads, O you gates,
          and be lifted up, you everlasting doors:
     and the King of glory shall come in.

8   Who is the King of glory?
     the Lord, strong and mighty, the Lord mighty in battle.

9   Lift up your heads, O you gates,
          and be lifted up, you everlasting doors:
     and the King of glory shall come in.

10   Who is the King of glory?
     the Lord of hosts, he is the King of glory.

or *Psalm 45.1–7*

1   My heart is astir with fine phrases,
          I make my song for a king:
     my tongue is the pen of a ready writer.

2   You are the fairest of the sons of men,
          grace flows from your lips:
     therefore has God blessed you for ever and ever.

3   Gird your sword upon your thigh, O mighty warrior:
     in glory and majesty tread down your foes, and triumph!

4   Ride on in the cause of truth:
      and for the sake of justice.

5   Your right hand shall teach a terrible instruction:
      peoples shall fall beneath you, your arrows shall be sharp
          in the hearts of the king's enemies.

6   Your throne is the throne of God, it endures for ever:
      and the sceptre of your kingdom is a righteous sceptre.

7   You have loved righteousness and hated evil:
      therefore God, your God, has anointed you
          with the oil of gladness above your fellows.

11   NEW TESTAMENT

1 Corinthians 1.18–25

The word of the cross is folly to those who are perishing, but
to us who are being saved it is the power of God. For it is
written,

'I will destroy the wisdom of the wise,
and the cleverness of the clever I will thwart.'

Where is the wise man? Where is the scribe? Where is
debater of this age? Has not God made foolish the wisdom of
the world? For since, in the wisdom of God, the world did not
know God through wisdom, it pleased God through the folly of
what we preach to save those who believe. For Jews demand
signs and Greeks seek wisdom, but we preach Christ crucified,
a stumbling block to Jews and folly to Gentiles, but to those
who are called, both Jews and Greeks, Christ the power of God
and the wisdom of God. For the foolishness of God is wiser
than men, and the weakness of God is stronger than men.

or *Hebrews 10.1–10*

Since the law has but a shadow of the good things to come
instead of the true form of these realities, it can never, by the
same sacrifices which are continually offered year after year,

make perfect those who draw near. Otherwise, would they not have ceased to be offered? If the worshippers had once been cleansed, they would no longer have any consciousness of sin. But in these sacrifices there is a reminder of sin year after year. For it is impossible that the blood of bulls and goats should take away sins.

Consequently, when Christ came into the world, he said,

'Sacrifices and offerings you have not desired,
but a body have you prepared for me;
in burnt offerings and sin offerings you have
    taken no pleasure.
Then I said, "Lo, I have come to do your will, O God,"
as it is written of me in the roll of the book.'

When he said above, 'You have neither desired nor taken pleasure in sacrifices and offerings and burnt offerings and sin offerings' (these are offered according to the law), then he added, 'Lo, I have come to do your will.' He abolishes the first in order to establish the second. And by that will we have been sanctified through the offering of the body of Jesus Christ once for all.

12 GOSPEL

The Gospel may be read in a dramatic form (see pp. 51 and 62).

Matthew 26.14—27 end

For a short version of this Gospel (Matt. 27. 11–54) start where indicated on page 39.

One of the twelve, who was called Judas Iscariot, went to the chief priests and said, 'What will you give me if I deliver him to you?' And they paid him thirty pieces of silver. And from that moment he sought an opportunity to betray him. Now on the first day of Unleavened Bread the disciples came to Jesus, saying, 'Where will you have us prepare for you to eat the passover?' He said, 'Go into the city to a certain one, and say to him, "The Teacher says, My time is at hand; I will keep the passover at your house with my disciples." ' And the disciples did as Jesus had directed them, and they prepared the passover.

When it was evening, he sat at table with the twelve disciples; and as they were eating, he said, 'Truly, I say to you, one of you will betray me.' And they were very sorrowful, and began to say to him one after another, 'Is it I, Lord?' He answered, 'He who has dipped his hand in the dish with me, will betray me. The Son of man goes as it is written of him, but woe to that man by whom the Son of man is betrayed! It would have been better for that man if he had not been born.' Judas, who betrayed him, said, 'Is it I, Master?' He said to him, 'You have said so.'

Now as they were eating, Jesus took bread, and blessed, and broke it, and gave it to the disciples and said, 'Take, eat; this is my body.' And he took a cup, and when he had given thanks he gave it to them, saying, 'Drink of it, all of you; for this is my blood of the covenant, which is poured out for many for the forgiveness of sins. I tell you I shall not drink again of this fruit of the vine until that day when I drink it new with you in my Father's kingdom.'

And when they had sung a hymn, they went out to the Mount of Olives. Then Jesus said to them, 'You will all fall away because of me this night; for it is written, "I will strike the shepherd, and the sheep of the flock will be scattered." But after I am raised up, I will go before you to Galilee.' Peter declared to him, 'Though they all fall away because of you, I will never fall away.' Jesus said to him, 'Truly, I say to you, this very night, before the cock crows, you will deny me three times.' Peter said to him, 'Even if I must die with you, I will not deny you.' And so said all the disciples.

Then Jesus went with them to a place called Gethsemane, and he said to his disciples, 'Sit here, while I go yonder and pray.' And taking with him Peter and the two sons of Zebedee, he began to be sorrowful and troubled. Then he said to them, 'My soul is very sorrowful, even to death; remain here, and watch with me.' And going a little farther he fell on his face and prayed, 'My Father, if it be possible, let this cup pass from me; nevertheless, not as I will, but as you will.' And he came to the disciples and found them sleeping; and he said to Peter, 'So, could you not watch with me one hour? Watch and pray that you may not enter into temptation; the spirit indeed is willing, but the flesh is weak.' Again, for the second time, he went away and prayed, 'My Father, if this cannot pass unless I drink it, your will be done.' And again he came and found them sleeping, for their eyes were heavy. So, leaving them again, he went away and prayed for the third time, saying the same words. Then he came to the disciples and said to them, 'Are you still sleeping and taking your rest? Behold, the hour is at hand, and the Son of man is betrayed into the hands of sinners. Rise, let us be going; see, my betrayer is at hand.'

While he was still speaking, Judas came, one of the twelve, and with him a great crowd with swords and clubs, from the chief priests and the elders of the people. Now the betrayer had given them a sign, saying, 'The one I shall kiss is the man; seize him.' And he came up to Jesus at once and said, 'Hail, Master!' And he kissed him. Jesus said to him, 'Friend, why are you here?' Then they came up and laid hands on Jesus and seized him. And behold, one of those who were with Jesus stretched out his hand and drew his sword, and struck the slave of the high priest, and cut off his ear. Then Jesus said to him, 'Put your sword back into its place; for all who take the sword will perish by the sword. Do you think that I cannot appeal to my Father, and he will at once send me more than twelve legions of angels? But how then should the scriptures be fulfilled, that it must be so?' At that hour Jesus said to the crowds, 'Have you come out as against a robber, with swords and clubs to capture me? Day after day I sat in the temple teaching and you did not seize me. But all this has taken place, that the scriptures of the prophets might be fulfilled.' Then all the disciples forsook him and fled.

Then those who had seized Jesus led him to Caiaphas the high priest, where the scribes and the elders had gathered. But Peter followed him at a distance, as far as the courtyard of the high priest, and going inside he sat with the guards to see the end. Now the chief priests and the whole council sought false testimony against Jesus that they might put him to death, but they found none, though many false witnesses came forward. At last two came forward and said, 'This fellow said, "I am able to destroy the temple of God, and to build it in three days." ' And the high priest stood up and said, 'Have you no answer to make? What is it that these men testify against you?' But Jesus was silent. And the high priest said to him, 'I adjure you by the living God, tell us if you are the Christ, the Son of God.' Jesus said to him, 'You have said so. But I tell you, hereafter you will see the Son of man seated at the right hand of Power, and coming on the clouds of heaven.' Then the high priest tore his robes, and said, 'He has uttered blasphemy. Why do we still need witnesses? You have now heard his blasphemy. What is your judgment?' They answered, 'He deserves death.' Then they spat in his face, and struck him; and some slapped him, saying, 'Prophesy to us, you Christ! Who is it that struck you?'

Now Peter was sitting outside in the courtyard. And a maid came up to him, and said, 'You also were with Jesus the Galilean.' But he denied it before them all, saying, 'I do not know what you mean.' And when he went out to the porch, another maid saw him, and she said to the bystanders, 'This man was with Jesus of Nazareth.' And again he denied it with an oath, 'I do not know the man.' After a little while the bystanders came up and said to Peter, 'Certainly you are also one of them, for your accent betrays you.' Then he began to invoke a curse on himself and to swear, 'I do not know the man.' And immediately the cock crowed. And Peter remembered the saying of Jesus, 'Before the cock crows, you will deny me three times.' And he went out and wept bitterly.

When morning came, all the chief priests and the elders of the people took counsel against Jesus to put him to death; and

they bound him and led him away and delivered him to Pilate
the governor.

When Judas, his betrayer, saw that he was condemned, he
repented and brought back the thirty pieces of silver to the
chief priests and the elders, saying, 'I have sinned in betraying
innocent blood.' They said, 'What is that to us? See to it
yourself.' And throwing down the pieces of silver in the
temple, he departed; and he went and hanged himself. But the
chief priests, taking the pieces of silver, said, 'It is not lawful to
put them into the treasury, since they are blood money.' So
they took counsel, and bought with them the potter's field, to
bury strangers in. Therefore that field has been called the Field
of Blood to this day. Then was fulfilled what had been spoken
by the prophet Jeremiah, saying, 'And they took the thirty
pieces of silver, the price of him on whom a price had been set
by some of the sons of Israel, and they gave them for the
potter's field, as the Lord directed me.'

(*Short version begins*)

Now Jesus stood before the governor; and the governor asked
him, 'Are you the King of the Jews?' Jesus said, 'You have
said so.' But when he was accused by the chief priests and
elders, he made no answer. Then Pilate said to him, 'Do you
not hear how many things they testify against you?' But
he gave him no answer, not even to a single charge; so that
the governor wondered greatly.

Now at the feast the governor was accustomed to release for
the crowd any one prisoner whom they wanted. And they had
then a notorious prisoner, called Barabbas. So when they had
gathered, Pilate said to them, 'Whom do you want me to
release for you, Barabbas or Jesus who is called Christ?' For he
knew that it was out of envy that they had delivered him up.
Besides, while he was sitting on the judgment seat, his wife
sent word to him, 'Have nothing to do with that righteous
man, for I have suffered much over him today in a dream.'
Now the chief priests and the elders persuaded the people to
ask for Barabbas and destroy Jesus. The governor again said to

them, 'Which of the two do you want me to release for you?'
And they said, 'Barabbas.' Pilate said to them, 'Then what
shall I do with Jesus who is called Christ?' They all said, 'Let
him be crucified.' And he said, 'Why, what evil has he done?'
But they shouted all the more, 'Let him be crucified.'

So when Pilate saw that he was gaining nothing, but rather
that a riot was beginning, he took water and washed his
hands before the crowd, saying, 'I am innocent of this man's
blood; see to it yourselves.' And all the people answered, 'His
blood be on us and on our children!' Then he released for
them Barabbas, and having scourged Jesus, delivered him to
be crucified.

Then the soldiers of the governor took Jesus into the
praetorium, and they gathered the whole battalion before him.
And they stripped him and put a scarlet robe upon him, and
plaiting a crown of thorns they put it on his head, and put a
reed in his right hand. And kneeling before him they mocked
him, saying, 'Hail, King of the Jews!' And they spat upon him,
and took the reed and struck him on the head. And when they
had mocked him, they stripped him of the robe, and put his
own clothes on him, and led him away to crucify him.

As they went out, they came upon a man of Cyrene,
Simon by name; this man they compelled to carry his cross.
And when they came to a place called Golgotha (which means
the place of a skull), they offered him wine to drink, mingled
with gall; but when he tasted it, he would not drink it. And
when they had crucified him, they divided his garments
among them by casting lots; then they sat down and kept
watch over him there. And over his head they put the charge
against him, which read, 'This is Jesus the King of the Jews.'
Then two robbers were crucified with him, one on the right
and one on the left. And those who passed by derided
him, wagging their heads and saying, 'You who would destroy
the temple and build it in three days, save yourself! If you are
the Son of God, come down from the cross.' So also the chief
priests, with the scribes and elders, mocked him, saying, 'He

saved others; he cannot save himself. He is the King of Israel;
let him come down now from the cross, and we will believe
in him. He trusts in God; let God deliver him now, if he desires
him; for he said, "I am the Son of God." ' And the robbers who
were crucified with him also reviled him in the same way.

Now from the sixth hour there was darkness over all the land
until the ninth hour. And about the ninth hour Jesus cried
with a loud voice, 'Eli, Eli, lama sabachthani?' that is, 'My God,
my God, why have you forsaken me?' And some of the
bystanders hearing it said, 'This man is calling Elijah.' And
one of them at once ran and took a sponge, filled it with
vinegar, and put it on a reed, and gave it to him to drink.
But the others said, 'Wait, let us see whether Elijah will come
to save him.' And Jesus cried again with a loud voice and
yielded up his spirit.

And behold, the curtain of the temple was torn in two, from
top to bottom; and the earth shook, and the rocks were split;
the tombs also were opened, and many bodies of the saints
who had fallen asleep were raised, and coming out of the
tombs after his resurrection they went into the holy city and
appeared to many. When the centurion and those who were
with him, keeping watch over Jesus, saw the earthquake and
what took place, they were filled with awe, and said, 'Truly
this was the son of God!'

(*Short version ends*)

There were also many women there, looking on from afar,
who had followed Jesus from Galilee, ministering to him;
among whom were Mary Magdalene, and Mary the mother of
James and Joseph, and the mother of the sons of Zebedee.

When it was evening, there came a rich man from Arimathea,
named Joseph, who also was a disciple of Jesus. He went to
Pilate and asked for the body of Jesus. Then Pilate ordered it to
be given to him. And Joseph took the body, and wrapped it in
a clean linen shroud, and laid it in his own new tomb, which
he had hewn in the rock; and he rolled a great stone to the

door of the tomb, and departed. Mary Magdalene and the other Mary were there, sitting opposite the sepulchre.

Next day, that is, after the day of Preparation, the chief priests and the Pharisees gathered before Pilate and said, 'Sir, we remember how that impostor said, while he was still alive, "After three days I will rise again." Therefore order the sepulchre to be made secure until the third day, lest his disciples go and steal him away, and tell the people, "He has risen from the dead," and the last fraud will be worse than the first.' Pilate said to them, 'You have a guard of soldiers; go, make it as secure as you can.' So they went and made the sepulchre secure by sealing the stone and setting a guard.

or *Mark 14 and 15*

For a short version of this Gospel (Mark 15.1–39) start where indicated on page 46.

It was now two days before the Passover and the feast of Unleavened Bread. And the chief priests and the scribes were seeking how to arrest Jesus by stealth, and kill him; for they said, 'Not during the feast, lest there be a tumult of the people.'

And while he was at Bethany in the house of Simon the leper, as he sat at table, a woman came with an alabaster flask of ointment of pure nard, very costly, and she broke the flask and poured it over his head. But there were some who said to themselves indignantly, 'Why was the ointment thus wasted? For this ointment might have been sold for more than three hundred denarii, and given to the poor.' And they reproached her. But Jesus said, 'Let her alone; why do you trouble her? She has done a beautiful thing to me. For you always have the poor with you, and whenever you will, you can do good to them; but you will not always have me. She has done what she could; she has anointed my body beforehand for burying. And truly, I say to you, wherever the gospel is preached in the whole world, what she has done will be told in memory of her.'

Then Judas Iscariot, who was one of the twelve, went to the chief priests in order to betray him to them. And when they heard it they were glad, and promised to give him money. And he sought an opportunity to betray him.

And on the first day of Unleavened Bread, when they sacrificed the passover lamb, his disciples said to him, 'Where will you have us go and prepare for you to eat the passover?' And he sent two of his disciples, and said to them, 'Go into the city, and a man carrying a jar of water will meet you; follow him, and wherever he enters, say to the householder, "The Teacher says, Where is my guest room, where I am to eat the passover with my disciples?" And he will show you a large upper room furnished and ready; there prepare for us.' And the disciples set out and went to the city, and found it as he had told them; and they prepared the passover.

And when it was evening he came with the twelve. And as they were at table eating, Jesus said, 'Truly, I say to you, one of you will betray me, one who is eating with me.' They began to be sorrowful, and to say to him one after another, 'Is it I?' He said to them, 'It is one of the twelve, one who is dipping bread into the dish with me. For the Son of man goes as it is written of him, but woe to that man by whom the Son of man is betrayed! It would have been better for that man if he had not been born.'

And as they were eating, he took bread, and blessed, and broke it, and gave it to them, and said, 'Take; this is my body.' And he took a cup, and when he had given thanks he gave it to them, and they all drank of it. And he said to them, 'This is my blood of the covenant, which is poured out for many. Truly, I say to you, I shall not drink again of the fruit of the vine until that day when I drink it new in the kingdom of God.'

And when they had sung a hymn, they went out to the Mount of Olives. And Jesus said to them, 'You will all fall away; for it is written, "I will strike the shepherd, and the sheep will be scattered." But after I am raised up, I will go before you to Galilee.' Peter said to him, 'Even though they all fall away, I will not.' And Jesus said to him, 'Truly, I say to you, this very night, before the cock crows twice, you will deny me three times.' But he said vehemently, 'If I must die with you, I will not deny you.' And they all said the same.

And they went to a place which was called Gethsemane; and he said to his disciples, 'Sit here, while I pray.' And he took with him Peter and James and John, and began to be greatly distressed and troubled. And he said to them, 'My soul is very sorrowful, even to death; remain here, and watch.' And going a little farther, he fell on the ground and prayed that, if it were possible, the hour might pass from him. And he said, 'Abba, Father, all things are possible to you; remove this cup from me; yet not what I will, but what you will.' And he came and found them sleeping, and he said to Peter, 'Simon, are you asleep? Could you not watch one hour? Watch and pray that you may not enter into temptation; the spirit indeed is willing, but the flesh is weak.' And again he went away and prayed, saying the same words. And again he came and found them sleeping, for their eyes were very heavy; and they did not know what to answer him. And he came the third time, and said to them, 'Are you still sleeping and taking your rest? It is enough; the hour has come; the Son of man is betrayed into the hands of sinners. Rise, let us be going; see, my betrayer is at hand.'

And immediately, while he was still speaking, Judas came, one of the twelve, and with him a crowd with swords and clubs, from the chief priests and the scribes and the elders. Now the betrayer had given them a sign, saying, 'The one I shall kiss is the man; seize him and lead him away under guard.' And when he came, he went up to him at once, and said, 'Master!' And he kissed him. And they laid hands on him and seized him. But one of those who stood by drew his sword, and struck the slave of the high priest and cut off his ear. And Jesus said to them, 'Have you come out as against a robber, with swords and clubs to capture me? Day after day I was with you in the temple teaching, and you did not seize me. But let the scriptures be fulfilled.' And they all forsook him, and fled.

And a young man followed him, with nothing but a linen cloth about his body; and they seized him, but he left the linen cloth and ran away naked.

And they led Jesus to the high priest; and all the chief priests and the elders and the scribes were assembled. And Peter had followed him at a distance, right into the courtyard of the high priest; and he was sitting with the guards, and warming himself at the fire. Now the chief priests and the whole council sought testimony against Jesus to put him to death; but they found none. For many bore false witness against him, and their witness did not agree. And some stood up and bore false witness against him, saying, 'We heard him say, "I will destroy this temple that is made with hands, and in three days I will build another, not made with hands."' Yet not even so did their testimony agree. And the high priest stood up in the midst, and asked Jesus, 'Have you no answer to make? What is it that these men testify against you?' But he was silent and made no answer. Again the high priest asked him, 'Are you the Christ, the Son of the Blessed?' And Jesus said, 'I am; and you will see the Son of man seated at the right hand of Power, and coming with the clouds of heaven.' And the high priest tore his garments, and said, 'Why do we still need witnesses? You have heard his blasphemy. What is your decision?' And they all condemned him as deserving death. And some began to spit on him, and to cover his face, and to strike him, saying to him, 'Prophesy!' And the guards received him with blows.

And as Peter was below in the courtyard, one of the maids of the high priest came; and seeing Peter warming himself, she looked at him, and said, 'You also were with the Nazarene, Jesus.' But he denied it, saying, 'I neither know nor understand what you mean.' And he went out into the gateway. And the maid saw him, and began again to say to the bystanders, 'This man is one of them.' But again he denied it. And after a little while again the bystanders said to Peter, 'Certainly you are one of them, for you are a Galilean.' But he began to invoke a curse on himself and to swear, 'I do not know this man of whom you speak.' And immediately the cock crowed a second time. And Peter remembered how Jesus had said to him, 'Before the cock crows twice, you will deny me three times.' And he broke down and wept.

(*Short version begins*)

As soon as it was morning the chief priests, with the elders and scribes, and the whole council held a consultation; and they bound Jesus and led him away and delivered him to Pilate. And Pilate asked him, 'Are you the King of the Jews?' And he answered him, 'You have said so.' And the chief priests accused him of many things. And Pilate again asked him, 'Have you no answer to make? See how many charges they bring against you.' But Jesus made no further answer, so that Pilate wondered.

Now at the feast he used to release for them one prisoner whom they asked. And among the rebels in prison, who had committed murder in the insurrection, there was a man called Barabbas. And the crowd came up and began to ask Pilate to do as he was wont to do for them. And he answered them, 'Do you want me to release for you the King of the Jews?' For he perceived that it was out of envy that the chief priests had delivered him up. But the chief priests stirred up the crowd to have him release for them Barabbas instead. And Pilate again said to them, 'Then what shall I do with the man whom you call the King of the Jews?' And they cried out again, 'Crucify him.' And Pilate said to them, 'Why, what evil has he done?' But they shouted all the more, 'Crucify him.' So Pilate, wishing to satisfy the crowd, released for them Barabbas; and having scourged Jesus, he delivered him to be crucified.

And the soldiers led him away inside the palace (that is, the praetorium); and they called together the whole battalion. And they clothed him in a purple cloak, and plaiting a crown of thorns they put it on him. And they began to salute him, 'Hail, King of the Jews!' And they struck his head with a reed, and spat upon him, and they knelt down in homage to him. And when they had mocked him, they stripped him of the purple cloak, and put his own clothes on him. And they led him out to crucify him.

And they compelled a passer-by, Simon of Cyrene, who was coming in from the country, the father of Alexander and Rufus, to carry his cross. And they brought him to the place called Golgotha (which means the place of a skull). And they offered him wine mingled with myrrh; but he did not take it. And they crucified him, and divided his garments among them, casting lots for them, to decide what each should take. And it was the third hour, when they crucified him. And the inscription of the charge against him read, 'The King of the Jews.' And with him they crucified two robbers, one on his right and one on his left. And those who passed by derided him, wagging their heads, and saying, 'Aha! You who would destroy the temple and build it in three days, save yourself, and come down from the cross!' So also the chief priests mocked him to one another with the scribes, saying, 'He saved others; he cannot save himself. Let the Christ, the King of Israel, come down now from the cross, that we may see and believe.' Those who were crucified with him also reviled him.

And when the sixth hour had come, there was darkness over the whole land until the ninth hour. And at the ninth hour Jesus cried with a loud voice, 'Eloi, Eloi, lama sabachthani?' which means, 'My God, my God, why have you forsaken me?' And some of the bystanders hearing it said, 'Behold, he is calling Elijah.' And one ran and, filling a sponge full of vinegar, put it on a reed and gave it to him to drink, saying, 'Wait, let us see whether Elijah will come to take him down.' And Jesus uttered a loud cry, and breathed his last. And the curtain of the temple was torn in two, from top to bottom. And when the centurion, who stood facing him, saw that he thus breathed his last, he said, 'Truly this man was the Son of God!'

(Short version ends)

There were also women looking on from afar, among whom were Mary Magdalene, and Mary the mother of James the younger and of Joses, and Salome, who, when he was in Galilee, followed him, and ministered to him; and also many other women who came up with him to Jerusalem.

And when evening had come, since it was the day of Preparation, that is, the day before the sabbath, Joseph of Arimathea, a respected member of the council, who was also himself looking for the kingdom of God, took courage and went to Pilate, and asked for the body of Jesus. And Pilate wondered if he were already dead; and summoning the centurion, he asked him whether he was already dead. And when he learned from the centurion that he was dead, he granted the body to Joseph. And he bought a linen shroud, and taking him down, wrapped him in the linen shroud, and laid him in a tomb which had been hewn out of the rock; and he rolled a stone against the door of the tomb. Mary Magdalene and Mary the mother of Joses saw where he was laid.

13   The rest of the main service follows, in its usual form.

N Narrator's part

✠ The words of Christ

R Third reader's part, comprising speeches of all other persons

C These words may be spoken by several speakers at once. This may be a group or the whole congregation.

The Passion of Our Lord Jesus Christ
according to Matthew *Matthew 26.14—27 end*

*(For a short version of this Passion start where indicated on
page 57.)*

N One of the twelve, who was called Judas Iscariot, went
to the chief priests and said,

R What will you give me if I deliver him to you?

N And they paid him thirty pieces of silver. And from that
moment he sought an opportunity to betray him.

Now on the first day of Unleavened Bread the disciples
came to Jesus, saying,

C Where will you have us prepare for you to eat the passover?

N He said,

✠ Go into the city to a certain one, and say to him, 'The
Teacher says, My time is at hand; I will keep the passover
at your house with my disciples.'

N And the disciples did as Jesus had directed them, and they
prepared the passover.

When it was evening, he sat at table with the twelve
disciples; and as they were eating, he said,

✠ Truly, I say to you, one of you will betray me.

N And they were very sorrowful, and began to say to him
one after another,

R Is it I, Lord?

N He answered,

✠ He who has dipped his hand in the dish with me, will
betray me. The Son of man goes as it is written of him,
but woe to that man by whom the Son of man is betrayed!

It would have been better for that man if he had not been born.

N Judas, who betrayed him, said,

R Is it I, Master?

N He said to him,

✠ You have said so.

N Now as they were eating, Jesus took bread, and blessed, and broke it, and gave it to the disciples, and said,

✠ Take, eat; this is my body.

N And he took a cup, and when he had given thanks he gave it to them, saying,

✠ Drink of it, all of you; for this is my blood of the covenant, which is poured out for many for the forgiveness of sins. I tell you I shall not drink again of this fruit of the vine until that day when I drink it new with you in my Father's kingdom.

N And when they had sung a hymn, they went out to the Mount of Olives.

Then Jesus said to them,

✠ You will all fall away because of me this night; for it is written, 'I will strike the shepherd, and the sheep of the flock will be scattered.' But after I am raised up, I will go before you to Galilee.

N Peter declared to him,

R Though they all fall away because of you, I will never fall away.

N Jesus said to him,

✠ Truly, I say to you, this very night, before the cock crows, you will deny me three times.

N Peter said to him,

R　Even if I must die with you, I will not deny you.

N　And so said all the disciples.

Then Jesus went with them to a place called Gethsemane, and he said to his disciples,

✠　Sit here, while I go yonder and pray.

N　And taking with him Peter and the two sons of Zebedee, he began to be sorrowful and troubled. Then he said to them,

✠　My soul is very sorrowful, even to death; remain here, and watch with me.

N　And going a little farther he fell on his face and prayed,

✠　My Father, if it be possible, let this cup pass from me; nevertheless, not as I will, but as you will.

N　And he came to the disciples and found them sleeping; and he said to Peter,

✠　So, could you not watch with me one hour? Watch and pray that you may not enter into temptation; the spirit indeed is willing, but the flesh is weak.

N　Again, for the second time, he went away and prayed,

✠　My Father, if this cannot pass unless I drink it, your will be done.

N　And again he came and found them sleeping, for their eyes were heavy. So, leaving them again, he went away and prayed for the third time, saying the same words. Then he came to the disciples and said to them,

✠　Are you still sleeping and taking your rest? Behold, the hour is at hand, and the Son of man is betrayed into the hands of sinners. Rise, let us be going; see, my betrayer is at hand.

N　While he was still speaking Judas came, one of the twelve, and with him a great crowd with swords and clubs, from the chief priests and the elders of the people. Now the betrayer had given them a sign, saying,

R The one I shall kiss is the man; seize him.

N And he came up to Jesus at once and said,

R Hail, Master!

N And he kissed him. Jesus said to him,

✛ Friend, why are you here?

N Then they came up and laid hands on Jesus and seized him. And behold, one of those who were with Jesus stretched out his hand and drew his sword, and struck the slave of the high priest, and cut off his ear. Then Jesus said to him,

✛ Put your sword back into its place; for all who take the sword will perish by the sword. Do you think that I cannot appeal to my Father, and he will at once send me more than twelve legions of angels? But how then should the scriptures be fulfilled, that it must be so?

N At that hour Jesus said to the crowds,

✛ Have you come out as against a robber, with swords and clubs to capture me? Day after day I sat in the temple teaching, and you did not seize me. But all this has taken place, that the scriptures of the prophets might be fulfilled.

N Then all the disciples forsook him and fled.

Then those who had seized Jesus led him to Caiaphas the high priest, where the scribes and the elders had gathered. But Peter followed him at a distance, as far as the courtyard of the high priest, and going inside he sat with the guards to see the end. Now the chief priests and the whole council sought false testimony against Jesus that they might put him to death, but they found none, though many false witnesses came forward. At last two came forward and said,

C This fellow said, 'I am able to destroy the temple of God, and to build it in three days.'

N And the high priest stood up and said,

R Have you no answer to make? What is it that these men testify against you?

N But Jesus was silent. And the high priest said to him,

R I adjure you by the living God, tell us if you are the Christ, the Son of God.

N Jesus said to him,

✠ You have said so. But I tell you, hereafter you will see the Son of man seated at the right hand of Power, and coming on the clouds of heaven.

N Then the high priest tore his robes, and said,

R He has uttered blasphemy. Why do we still need witnesses? You have now heard his blasphemy. What is your judgment?

N They answered,

C He deserves death.

N Then they spat in his face, and struck him; and some slapped him, saying,

C Prophesy to us, you Christ! Who is it that struck you?

N Now Peter was sitting outside in the courtyard. And a maid came to him, and said,

R You also were with Jesus the Galilean.

N But he denied it before them all, saying,

R I do not know what you mean.

N And when he went out to the porch, another maid saw him, and she said to the bystanders,

R This man was with Jesus of Nazareth.

N And again he denied it with an oath,

R I do not know the man.

N After a little while the bystanders came up and said to Peter,

C Certainly you are also one of them, for your accent betrays you.

N Then he began to invoke a curse on himself and to swear,

R I do not know the man.

N And immediately the cock crowed. And Peter remembered the saying of Jesus, 'Before the cock crows, you will deny me three times.' And he went out and wept bitterly.

When morning came, all the chief priests and the elders of the people took counsel against Jesus to put him to death; and they bound him and led him away and delivered him to Pilate the governor.

When Judas, his betrayer, saw that he was condemned, he repented and brought back the thirty pieces of silver to the chief priests and the elders, saying,

R I have sinned in betraying innocent blood.

N They said,

C What is that to us? See to it yourself.

N And throwing down the pieces of silver in the temple, he departed; and he went and hanged himself. But the chief priests, taking the pieces of silver, said,

C It is not lawful to put them into the treasury, since they are blood money.

N So they took counsel, and bought with them the potter's field, to bury strangers in. Therefore that field has been called the Field of Blood to this day. Then was fulfilled what had been spoken by the prophet Jeremiah, saying, 'And they took the thirty pieces of silver, the price of him on

whom a price had been set by some of the sons of Israel,
and they gave them for the potter's field, as the Lord
directed me.'

(*Short version begins*)

N   Now Jesus stood before the governor; and the governor
    asked him,

R   Are you the King of the Jews?

N   Jesus said,

✠   You have said so.

N   But when he was accused by the chief priests and elders,
    he made no answer. Then Pilate said to him,

R   Do you not hear how many things they testify against you?

N   But he gave him no answer, not even to a single charge; so
    that the governor wondered greatly.

    Now at the feast the governor was accustomed to release
    for the crowd any one prisoner whom they wanted. And
    they had then a notorious prisoner, called Barabbas. So
    when they had gathered, Pilate said to them,

R   Whom do you want me to release for you, Barabbas or
    Jesus who is called Christ?

N   For he knew that it was out of envy that they had
    delivered him up. Besides, while he was sitting on the
    judgment seat, his wife sent word to him,

R   Have nothing to do with that righteous man, for I have
    suffered much over him today in a dream.

N   Now the chief priests and the elders persuaded the people
    to ask for Barabbas and destroy Jesus. The governor again
    said to them,

R   Which of the two do you want me to release for you?

N   And they said,

C   Barabbas.

N   Pilate said to them,

R   Then what shall I do with Jesus who is called Christ?

N   They all said,

C   Let him be crucified.

N   And he said,

R   Why, what evil has he done?

N   But they shouted all the more,

C   Let him be crucified.

N   So when Pilate saw that he was gaining nothing, but rather that a riot was beginning, he took water and washed his hands before the crowd, saying

R   I am innocent of this man's blood; see to it yourselves.

N   And all the people answered,

C   His blood be on us and on our children!

N   Then he released for them Barabbas, and having scourged Jesus, delivered him to be crucified.

Then the soldiers of the governor took Jesus into the praetorium, and they gathered the whole battalion before him. And they stripped him and put a scarlet robe upon him, and plaiting a crown of thorns they put it on his head, and put a reed in his right hand. And kneeling before him they mocked him, saying,

C   Hail, King of the Jews!

N   And they spat upon him, and took the reed and struck him on the head. And when they had mocked him, they stripped him of the robe, and put his own clothes on him, and led him away to crucify him.

As they went out, they came upon a man of Cyrene, Simon by name; this man they compelled to carry his cross. And when they came to a place called Golgotha (which means the place of a skull), they offered him wine to drink, mingled with gall; but when he tasted it, he would not drink it. And when they had crucified him, they divided his garments among them by casting lots; then they sat down and kept watch over him there. And over his head they put the charge against him, which read, 'This is Jesus the King of the Jews.' Then two robbers were crucified with him, one on the right and one on the left. And those who passed by derided him, wagging their heads and saying,

C   You who would destroy the temple and build it in three days, save yourself! If you are the Son of God, come down from the cross.

N   So also the chief priests, with the scribes and elders, mocked him, saying,

C   He saved others; he cannot save himself. He is the King of Israel; let him come down now from the cross, and we will believe in him. He trusts in God; let God deliver him now, if he desires him; for he said, 'I am the Son of God.'

N   And the robbers who were crucified with him also reviled him in the same way.

Now from the sixth hour there was darkness over all the land until the ninth hour. And about the ninth hour Jesus cried with a loud voice,

✠   Eli, Eli, lama sabachthani?

N   That is,

✠   My God, my God, why have you forsaken me?

N   And some of the bystanders hearing it said,

C   This man is calling Elijah.

N   And one of them at once ran and took a sponge, filled it
    with vinegar, and put it on a reed, and gave it to him to
    drink. But the others said,

C   Wait, let us see whether Elijah will come to save him.

N   And Jesus cried again with a loud voice and yielded up his
    spirit.

    And behold, the curtain of the temple was torn in two, from
    top to bottom; and the earth shook, and the rocks were
    split; the tombs also were opened, and many bodies of the
    saints who had fallen asleep were raised, and coming out
    of the tombs after his resurrection they went into the holy
    city and appeared to many. When the centurion and those
    who were with him, keeping watch over Jesus, saw the
    earthquake and what took place, they were filled with awe,
    and said,

C   Truly this was the Son of God!

(Short version ends)

N   There were also many women there, looking on from afar,
    who had followed Jesus from Galilee, ministering to him;
    among whom were Mary Magdalene, and Mary the mother
    of James and Joseph, and the mother of the sons of
    Zebedee.

    When it was evening, there came a rich man from
    Arimathea, named Joseph, who also was a disciple of Jesus.
    He went to Pilate and asked for the body of Jesus. Then
    Pilate ordered it to be given to him. And Joseph took the
    body, and wrapped it in a clean linen shroud, and laid it
    in his own new tomb, which he had hewn in the rock;
    and he rolled a great stone to the door of the tomb, and
    departed. Mary Magdalene and the other Mary were there,
    sitting opposite the sepulchre.

    Next day, that is, after the day of Preparation, the chief
    priests and the Pharisees gathered before Pilate and said,

C   Sir, we remember how that impostor said, while he was
    still alive, 'After three days I will rise again.' Therefore
    order the sepulchre to be made secure until the third day,
    lest his disciples go and steal him away, and tell the people,
    'He has risen from the dead,' and the last fraud will be
    worse than the first.

N   Pilate said to them,

R   You have a guard of soldiers; go, make it as secure as you
    can.

N   So they went and made the sepulchre secure by sealing the
    stone and setting a guard.

The Passion of Our Lord Jesus Christ according to Mark *Mark 14 and 15*

For a short version of this Passion start where indicated on page 67.

N It was now two days before the Passover and the feast of Unleavened Bread. And the chief priests and the scribes were seeking how to arrest Jesus by stealth, and kill him; for they said,

C Not during the feast, lest there be a tumult of the people.

N And while he was at Bethany in the house of Simon the leper, as he sat at table, a woman came with an alabaster flask of ointment of pure nard, very costly, and she broke the flask and poured it over his head. But there were some who said to themselves indignantly,

C Why was the ointment thus wasted? For this ointment might have been sold for more than three hundred denarii, and given to the poor.

N And they reproached her. But Jesus said,

✠ Let her alone; why do you trouble her? She has done a beautiful thing to me. For you always have the poor with you, and whenever you will, you can do good to them; but you will not always have me. She has done what she could; she has anointed my body beforehand for burying. And truly, I say to you, wherever the gospel is preached in the whole world, what she has done will be told in memory of her.

N Then Judas Iscariot, who was one of the twelve, went to the chief priests in order to betray him to them. And when they heard it they were glad, and promised to give him money. And he sought an opportunity to betray him.

And on the first day of Unleavened Bread, when they sacrificed the passover lamb, his disciples said to him,

Shorter edition page 20

C   Where will you have us go and prepare for you to eat the passover?

N   And he sent two of his disciples, and said to them,

✠   Go into the city, and a man carrying a jar of water will meet you; follow him, and wherever he enters, say to the householder, 'The Teacher says, Where is my guest room, where I am to eat the passover with my disciples?' And he will show you a large upper room furnished and ready; there prepare for us.

N   And the disciples set out and went to the city, and found it as he had told them; and they prepared the passover. And when it was evening he came with the twelve. And as they were at table eating, Jesus said,

✠   Truly, I say to you, one of you will betray me, one who is eating with me.

N   They began to be sorrowful, and to say to him one after another,

R   Is it I?

N   He said to them,

✠   It is one of the twelve, one who is dipping bread into the dish with me. For the Son of man goes as it is written of him, but woe to that man by whom the Son of man is betrayed! It would have been better for that man if he had not been born.

N   And as they were eating, he took bread, and blessed, and broke it, and gave it to them, and said,

✠   Take; this is my body.

N   And he took a cup, and when he had given thanks he gave it to them, and they all drank of it. And he said to them,

✠   This is my blood of the covenant, which is poured out for many. Truly, I say to you, I shall not drink again of the fruit of the vine until that day when I drink it new in the kingdom of God.

N And when they had sung a hymn, they went out to the Mount of Olives. And Jesus said to them,

✠ You will all fall away; for it is written, 'I will strike the shepherd, and the sheep will be scattered.' But after I am raised up, I will go before you to Galilee.

N Peter said to him,

R Even though they all fall away, I will not.

N And Jesus said to him,

✠ Truly, I say to you, this very night, before the cock crows twice, you will deny me three times.

N But he said vehemently,

R If I must die with you, I will not deny you.

N And they all said the same.

And they went to a place which was called Gethsemane; and he said to his disciples,

✠ Sit here, while I pray.

N And he took with him Peter and James and John, and began to be greatly distressed and troubled. And he said to them,

✠ My soul is very sorrowful, even to death; remain here, and watch.

N And going a little farther, he fell on the ground and prayed that, if it were possible, the hour might pass from him. And he said,

✠ Abba, Father, all things are possible to you; remove this cup from me; yet not what I will, but what you will.

N And he came and found them sleeping, and he said to Peter,

✠ Simon, are you asleep? Could you not watch one hour? Watch and pray that you may not enter into temptation; the spirit indeed is willing, but the flesh is weak.

N And again he went away and prayed, saying the same words. And again he came and found them sleeping, for their eyes were very heavy; and they did not know what to answer him. And he came the third time, and said to them,

✠ Are you still sleeping and taking your rest? It is enough; the hour has come; the Son of man is betrayed into the hands of sinners. Rise, let us be going; see, my betrayer is at hand.

N And immediately, while he was still speaking, Judas came, one of the twelve, and with him a crowd with swords and clubs, from the chief priests and the scribes and the elders. Now the betrayer had given them a sign, saying,

R The one I shall kiss is the man; seize him and lead him away under guard.

N And when he came, he went up to him at once, and said,

R Master!

N And he kissed him. And they laid hands on him and seized him. But one of those who stood by drew his sword, and struck the slave of the high priest and cut off his ear. And Jesus said to them,

✠ Have you come out as against a robber, with swords and clubs to capture me? Day after day I was with you in the temple teaching, and you did not seize me. But let the scriptures be fulfilled.

N And they all forsook him, and fled. And a young man followed him, with nothing but a linen cloth about his body; and they seized him, but he left the linen cloth and ran away naked.

And they led Jesus to the high priest; and all the chief priests and the elders and the scribes were assembled. And Peter had followed him at a distance, right into the courtyard of the high priest; and he was sitting with the guards, and warming himself at the fire. Now the chief priests and the whole council sought testimony against Jesus to put him to death; but they found none. For many bore false witness against him, and their witness did not agree. And some stood up and bore false witness against him, saying,

C We heard him say, 'I will destroy this temple that is made with hands, and in three days I will build another, not made with hands.'

N Yet not even so did their testimony agree. And the high priest stood up in the midst, and asked Jesus,

R Have you no answer to make? What is it that these men testify against you?

N But he was silent and made no answer. Again the high priest asked him,

R Are you the Christ, the Son of the Blessed?

N And Jesus said,

✠ I am; and you will see the Son of man seated at the right hand of Power, and coming with the clouds of heaven.

N And the high priest tore his garments, and said,

R Why do we still need witnesses? You have heard his blasphemy. What is your decision?

N And they all condemned him as deserving death. And some began to spit on him, and to cover his face, and to strike him, saying to him,

C Prophesy!

N And the guards received him with blows.

And as Peter was below in the courtyard, one of the maids of the high priest came; and seeing Peter warming himself, she looked at him, and said,

R   You also were with the Nazarene, Jesus.

N   But he denied it, saying,

R   I neither know nor understand what you mean.

N   And he went out into the gateway. And the maid saw him, and began again to say to the bystanders,

R   This man is one of them.

N   But again he denied it. And after a little while again the bystanders said to Peter,

C   Certainly you are one of them; for you are a Galilean.

N   But he began to invoke a curse on himself and to swear,

R   I do not know this man of whom you speak.

N   And immediately the cock crowed a second time. And Peter remembered how Jesus had said to him, 'Before the cock crows twice, you will deny me three times.' And he broke down and wept.

(*Short version begins*)

N   As soon as it was morning the chief priests, with the elders and scribes, and the whole council held a consultation; and they bound Jesus and led him away and delivered him to Pilate. And Pilate asked him,

R   Are you the King of the Jews?

N   And he answered him,

✠   You have said so.

N   And the chief priests accused him of many things. And Pilate again asked him,

R   Have you no answer to make? See how many charges they bring against you.

N   But Jesus made no further answer, so that Pilate wondered.

Now at the feast he used to release for them one prisoner for whom they asked. And among the rebels in prison, who had committed murder in the insurrection, there was a man called Barabbas. And the crowd came up and began to ask Pilate to do as he was wont to do for them. And he answered them,

R   Do you want me to release for you the King of the Jews?

N   For he perceived that it was out of envy that the chief priests had delivered him up. But the chief priests stirred up the crowd to have him release for them Barabbas instead. And Pilate again said to them,

R   Then what shall I do with the man whom you call the King of the Jews?

N   And they cried out again,

C   Crucify him.

N   And Pilate said to them,

R   Why, what evil has he done?

N   But they shouted all the more,

C   Crucify him.

N   So Pilate, wishing to satisfy the crowd, released for them Barabbas; and having scourged Jesus, he delivered him to be crucified.

And the soldiers led him away inside the palace (that is, the praetorium); and they called together the whole battalion. And they clothed him in a purple cloak, and plaiting a crown of thorns they put it on him. And they began to salute him,

C   Hail, King of the Jews!

N   And they struck his head with a reed, and spat upon him, and they knelt down in homage to him. And when they had mocked him, they stripped him of the purple cloak, and put his own clothes on him. And they led him out to crucify him.

And they compelled a passer-by, Simon of Cyrene, who was coming in from the country, the father of Alexander and Rufus, to carry his cross. And they brought him to the place called Golgotha (which means the place of a skull). And they offered him wine mingled with myrrh; but he did not take it. And they crucified him, and divided his garments among them, casting lots for them, to decide what each should take. And it was the third hour, when they crucified him. And the inscription of the charge against him read, 'The King of the Jews.' And with him they crucified two robbers, one on his right and one on his left. And those who passed by derided him, wagging their heads, and saying,

C   Aha! You who would destroy the temple and build it in three days, save yourself, and come down from the cross!

N   So also the chief priests mocked him to one another with the scribes, saying,

C   He saved others; he cannot save himself. Let the Christ, the King of Israel, come down now from the cross, that we may see and believe.

N   Those who were crucified with him also reviled him.

And when the sixth hour had come, there was darkness over the whole land until the ninth hour. And at the ninth hour Jesus cried with a loud voice,

✠   Eloi, Eloi, lama sabachthani?

N   Which means,

✠   My God, my God, why have you forsaken me?

N   And some of the bystanders hearing it said,

C   Behold, he is calling Elijah.

69

N   And one ran and, filling a sponge full of vinegar, put it on
     a reed and gave it to him to drink, saying,

R   Wait, let us see whether Elijah will come to take him down.

N   And Jesus uttered a loud cry, and breathed his last. And
     the curtain of the temple was torn in two, from top to
     bottom. And when the centurion, who stood facing him,
     saw that he thus breathed his last, he said,

R   Truly this man was the Son of God!

(*Short version ends*)

N   There were also women looking on from afar, among whom
     were Mary Magdalene, and Mary the mother of James
     the younger and of Joses, and Salome, who, when he
     was in Galilee, followed him, and ministered to him; and also
     many other women who came up with him to Jerusalem.

     And when evening had come, since it was the day of
     Preparation, that is, the day before the sabbath, Joseph of
     Arimathea, a respected member of the council, who was
     also himself looking for the kingdom of God, took courage
     and went to Pilate, and asked for the body of Jesus. And
     Pilate wondered if he were already dead; and summoning
     the centurion, he asked him whether he was already dead.
     And when he learned from the centurion that he was
     dead, he granted the body to Joseph. And he bought a
     linen shroud, and taking him down, wrapped him in the
     linen shroud, and laid him in a tomb which had been
     hewn out of the rock; and he rolled a stone against the
     door of the tomb. Mary Magdalene and Mary the mother
     of Joses saw where he was laid.

MONDAY

Penitence

1 SENTENCE

> We have Jesus Christ to plead our cause with the Father,
> and he is just. He is the sacrifice that takes away, not
> only our own sins, but the sins of the whole world.

2 HYMN

3 THE TEN COMMANDMENTS

> Our Lord Jesus Christ said, If you love me, keep my
> commandments; happy are those who hear the word of
> God and keep it. Hear then these commandments which
> God has given to his people, and take them to heart.

> I am the Lord your God: you shall have no other gods
> but me.
> You shall love the Lord your God with all your heart,
> with all your soul, with all your mind and with all your
> strength.
> **Amen. Lord, have mercy.**

> You shall not make for yourself any idol.
> God is spirit, and those who worship him must worship
> in spirit and in truth.
> **Amen. Lord, have mercy.**

> You shall not dishonour the name of the Lord your God.
> You shall worship him with awe and reverence.
> **Amen. Lord, have mercy.**

> Remember the Lord's day and keep it holy.
> Christ is risen from the dead: set your minds on things
> that are above, not on things that are on the earth.
> **Amen. Lord, have mercy.**

Honour your father and mother.
Live as servants of God; honour all men; love the
brotherhood.
Amen. Lord, have mercy.

You shall not commit murder.
Be reconciled to your brother, overcome evil with good.
Amen. Lord, have mercy.

You shall not commit adultery.
Know that your body is a temple of the Holy Spirit.
Amen. Lord, have mercy.

You shall not steal.
Be honest in all that you do and care for those in need.
Amen. Lord, have mercy.

You shall not be a false witness.
Let everyone speak the truth.
Amen. Lord, have mercy.

You shall not covet anything which belongs to your
neighbour.
Remember the words of the Lord Jesus: It is more blessed
to give than to receive. Love your neighbour as yourself,
for love is the fulfilling of the law.
Amen. Lord, have mercy.

4   SILENCE FOR SELF-EXAMINATION

5   THE CONFESSION

Have mercy on us, O God, in your goodness;
in your great tenderness wipe away our faults.
Wash us clean of our guilt,
Purify us from our sin.
God, create a clean heart in us,
put into us a new and constant spirit;
Be our saviour again, renew our joy,
Keep our spirit steady and willing.

5   THE DECLARATION FOR FORGIVENESS

> The almighty and merciful God grant us pardon and
> remission of all our sins, time for amendment of life, and
> the grace and comfort of the Holy Spirit. **Amen.**

7   A LITANY

> From pride, envy and resentment; and from a refusal to
> love our neighbour
> **Good Lord, deliver us.**
>
> From lust, evil thoughts; and the wrongful indulgence in
> bodily desires
> **Good Lord, deliver us.**
>
> From indifference to the needs of others; and a refusal to
> use the gifts entrusted to our charge
> **Good Lord, deliver us.**
>
> From greed, dishonesty, and selfishness; and from all
> injustice to others
> **Good Lord, deliver us.**
>
> From deeds and attitudes that deny our common
> humanity; and from all misuse of God's creation
> **Good Lord, deliver us.**

8   The main service of the day follows, beginning with the
Collect:

> Almighty and everlasting God,
> you hate nothing that you have made
> and forgive the sins of all those who are penitent.
> Create and make in us new and contrite hearts,
> that, lamenting our sins
>   and acknowledging our wretchedness,
> we may receive from you, the God of all mercy,
> perfect forgiveness and peace;
> through Jesus Christ our Lord. **Amen.**

9   READINGS

Year 1	Year 2
Isaiah 42.1–4	*Lamentations 3.19–33*
Acts 10.34–43	*Philippians 2.1–13*
Mark 14.1–26	*Luke 22.1–38*

Psalms 130; 79.8–10

10 If there is no communion, the service ends with the sermon, prayers of thanksgiving and intercession, and the following:

To God the Father, who first loved us, and made us accepted in the Beloved:
To God the Son, who loved us, and washed us from our sins in his own blood:
To God the Holy Spirit, who sheds the love of God abroad in our hearts:
Be all love and glory for time and for eternity. **Amen.**

Alternative Service

The Day of Cleansing

1   Today we remember that our Lord cleansed the temple,
     and declared that his Father's house should be a house of
     prayer for all nations.

2 SENTENCE

     Jesus said: How blest are those who hunger and thirst to
     see right prevail; they shall be satisfied.

3 HYMN

4 PRAYER

     Almighty and everlasting God,
     who in your tender love towards mankind
         sent your Son our Saviour Jesus Christ
     to take upon him our flesh
     and to suffer death upon the cross:
     grant that we may follow the example
         of his patience and humility,
     and also be made partakers of his resurrection;
     through Jesus Christ our Lord. **Amen.**

   or

     Almighty God,
     whose most dear Son went not up to joy
         but first he suffered pain,
     and entered not into glory before he was crucified:
     mercifully grant that we, walking in the way of the cross,
     may find it none other than the way of life and peace;
     through Jesus Christ your Son our Lord,
     who is alive and reigns with you and the Holy Spirit,
     one God, for ever and ever. **Amen.**

Shorter edition page 32

5   OLD TESTAMENT

Jeremiah 7.1–15

The word that came to Jeremiah from the Lord: 'Stand in the gate of the Lord's house, and proclaim there this word, and say, Hear the word of the Lord, all you men of Judah who enter these gates to worship the Lord. Thus says the Lord of hosts, the God of Israel, Amend your ways and your doings, and I will let you dwell in this place. Do not trust in these deceptive words: "This is the temple of the Lord, the temple of the Lord, the temple of the Lord."

'For if you truly amend your ways and your doings, if you truly execute justice one with another, if you do not oppress the alien, the fatherless or the widow, or shed innocent blood in this place, and if you do not go after other gods to your own hurt, then I will let you dwell in this place, in the land that I gave of old to your fathers for ever.

'Behold, you trust in deceptive words to no avail. Will you steal, murder, commit adultery, swear falsely, burn incense to Baal, and go after other gods that you have not known, and then come and stand before me in this house, which is called by my name, and say, "We are delivered!" – only to go on doing all these abominations? Has this house, which is called by my name, become a den of robbers in your eyes? Behold, I myself have seen it, says the Lord. Go now to my place that was in Shiloh, where I made my name dwell at first, and see what I did to it for the wickedness of my people Israel. And now, because you have done all these things, says the Lord, and when I spoke to you persistently you did not listen, and when I called you, you did not answer, therefore I will do to the house which is called by my name, and in which you trust, and to the place which I gave to you and to your fathers, as I did to Shiloh. And I will cast you out of my sight, as I cast out all your kinsmen, all the offspring of Ephraim.'

or *Isaiah 56.6–8*

The foreigners who join themselves to the Lord,
   to minister to him, to love the name of the Lord,
   and to be his servants,
every one who keeps the sabbath, and does not profane it,
   and holds fast my covenant –
these I will bring to my holy mountain,
   and make them joyful in my house of prayer;
their burnt offerings and their sacrifices
   will be accepted on my altar;
for my house shall be called a house of prayer
   for all peoples.
Thus says the Lord God,
   who gathers the outcasts of Israel,
I will gather yet others to him
   besides those already gathered.

The following psalm, or a hymn.

Psalm 26

1 Give judgement for me, O Lord,
    for I have walked in my integrity:
   I have trusted in the Lord and not wavered.

2 Put me to the test, O Lord; and prove me:
   try my mind and my heart.

3 For your steadfast love has been ever before my eyes:
   and I have walked in your truth.

4 I have not sat with deceivers:
   nor consorted with the hypocrites;

5 I hate the assembly of the wicked:
   I will not sit with the ungodly.

6 I wash my hands in innocence, O Lord:
   that I may go about your altar,

7 And lift up the voice of thanksgiving:
to tell of all your marvellous works.

8 Lord, I love the house of your habitation:
and the place where your glory dwells.

9 Do not sweep me away with sinners:
nor my life with men of blood,

10 In whose hand is abomination:
and their right hand is full of bribes.

11 As for me, I walk in my integrity:
O ransom me and be favourable toward me.

12 My foot stands on an even path:
I will bless the Lord in the great congregation.

7   GOSPEL

Mark 11.12–26

On the following day, when Jesus and his disciples came from
Bethany, he was hungry. And seeing in the distance a fig tree
in leaf, he went to see if he could find anything on it. When he
came to it, he found nothing but leaves, for it was not the
season for figs. And he said to it, 'May no one ever eat fruit
from you again.' And his disciples heard it.

And they came to Jerusalem. And he entered the temple and
began to drive out those who sold and those who bought in
the temple, and he overturned the tables of the money-
changers and the seats of those who sold pigeons; and he
would not allow any one to carry anything through the
temple. And he taught, and said to them, 'Is it not written, "My
house shall be called a house of prayer for all the nations"?
But you have made it a den of robbers.' And the chief priests
and the scribes heard it and sought a way to destroy him; for
they feared him, because all the multitude was astonished at
his teaching. And when evening came they went out of the
city.

As they passed by in the morning, they saw the fig tree withered away to its roots. And Peter remembered and said to him, 'Master, look! The fig tree which you cursed has withered.' And Jesus answered them, 'Have faith in God. Truly, I say to you, whoever says to this mountain. "Be taken up and cast into the sea," and does not doubt in his heart, but believes that what he says will come to pass, it will be done for him. Therefore I tell you, whatever you ask in prayer, believe that you receive it, and you will. And whenever you stand praying, forgive, if you have anything against any one; so that your Father also who is in heaven may forgive you your trespasses.'

or *Luke 19.41–48*

When Jesus drew near and saw the city he wept over it, saying, 'Would that even today you knew the things that make for peace! But now they are hid from your eyes. For the days shall come upon you, when your enemies will cast up a bank about you and surround you, and hem you in on every side, and dash you to the ground, you and your children within you, and they will not leave one stone upon another in you; because you did not know the time of your visitation.' And he entered the temple and began to drive out those who sold, saying to them, 'It is written, "My house shall be a house of prayer"; but you have made it a den of robbers.'

And he was teaching daily in the temple. The chief priests and the scribes and the principal men of the people sought to destroy him; but they did not find anything they could do, for all the people hung upon his words.

8   SERMON

9   THANKSGIVING

> Eternal God, we praise you
> that beyond the beauty of this earth
> we can see your eternal glory.

We praise you
that through Christ you have opened for us sinners
the way of salvation.
We thank you for the love and humility
with which he came to live among us,
wept over Jerusalem,
cleansed the temple
that it might be a house of prayer for all the nations,
was crucified, died and was buried.
On the third day he rose from the dead;
he ascended into heaven,
and there he pleads for us.

Accept our praises,
cleanse our hearts from sin
and fill them with the spirit of prayer
that they may be fit temples of your Holy Spirit.
Bring forth in us, we pray, the fruit of good works
that on the day of Christ's triumph
we may be presented blameless before him,
to whom be the glory for ever. **Amen.**

Or, if a Eucharist is to follow, this prayer may be said here:

Almighty God,
whose son Jesus Christ purged the temple courts
purify our hearts from all defilement,
    our worship from all insincerity
    and our lives from all hypocrisy,
that we may become your temple,
fit dwelling places for the Holy Spirit.
Forgive the ways in which we have betrayed our calling
and restore us to a fruitful life of service and integrity;
through Jesus Christ our Lord. **Amen.**

10   Intercession may follow here, particularly for the Church.

11   If there is no Eucharist, the service concludes with the Lord's
Prayer, a hymn and the Dismissal.

80

TUESDAY

Obedience

1   SENTENCE

> Christ Jesus humbled himself and in obedience accepted
> even death, death on a cross.

2   HYMN

3   COLLECT

> Father, you have appointed our Lord Jesus Christ
>   as Mediator of a new covenant:
> give us grace to draw near with fullness of faith
> and join ourselves in a perpetual covenant with you;
> through Jesus Christ our Lord. **Amen.**

4   READINGS

> Year 1   Year 2
> *Isaiah 49.1–6*   *Genesis 22.1–12*
> *Hebrews 4.14—5.10* *Colossians 2.6–15*
> *Mark 14.27–42*   *Luke 22.39–71*
>
> *Psalms 69.16–21; 35.11–16*

5   SERMON

6   HYMN

7   THE RENEWAL OF THE COVENANT

All remain standing while the Minister says:

> In the Old Covenant, God chose Israel to be his people
> and to obey his laws. Our Lord Jesus Christ, by his death
> and resurrection, has given a New Covenant to all who

trust in him. We stand within this Covenant and we bear his name.

On the one side, God promises to give us new life in Christ.

On the other side, we are pledged to live no more for ourselves but for him.

Let us now renew our part in this Covenant which God has made with his people, and take the yoke of Christ upon us.

Christ has many services to be done; some are easy, others are difficult; some bring honour, others bring reproach; some are suitable to our natural inclinations and material interests, others are contrary to both. In some we may please Christ and please ourselves, in others we cannot please Christ except by denying ourselves. Yet the power to do all these things is given us in Christ who strengthens us.

Lord God,
in our baptism
you called us and brought us into your Church,
commissioning us to witness to the faith
    of the crucified Christ
and to be his faithful disciples
    to the end of our lives;
so now
with joy we take upon ourselves the yoke of obedience
and for love of you engage ourselves
to seek and do your perfect will.
We are no longer our own, but yours.

The people say:

I am no longer my own, but yours. Put me to what you will, rank me with whom you will; put me to doing, put me to suffering; let me be employed for you or laid aside for you, exalted for you or brought low for you; let me be full, let me be empty; let me have all things, let me have nothing; I freely and wholeheartedly yield all things to your pleasure and disposal.

And now, glorious and blessed God, Father, Son and Holy Spirit, you are mine and I am yours. So be it. And the covenant which I have made on earth, let it be ratified in heaven.

8   The Baptismal Creed may be said.

> I believe in God, the Father almighty,
>   creator of heaven and earth.
>
> I believe in Jesus Christ, his only Son, our Lord.
>   He was conceived by the power of the Holy Spirit
>   and born of the Virgin Mary.
>   He suffered under Pontius Pilate,
>   was crucified, died and was buried.
>   He descended to the dead.
>   On the third day he rose again.
>   He ascended into heaven,
>   and is seated at the right hand of the Father.
>   He will come again to judge the living and the dead.
>
> I believe in the Holy Spirit,
>   the holy catholic Church,
>   the communion of saints,
>   the forgiveness of sins,
>   the resurrection of the body,
>   and the life everlasting.

9   INTERCESSIONS

These should include the following:
    for those under instruction in the faith;
    for those who are preparing for baptism or confirmation;
    for the children of the Church and for those responsible for
        them . . .

83

10   The rest of the Eucharist now follows.

or

11   If there is no communion, the service ends after the prayers
with the following:

>   Almighty, eternal God,
>   we thank you that your Son
>   accepted the baptism of forgiveness,
>   identified himself with men
>   and has given us an example of true humility
>   and unconquerable obedience:
>   we thank you that you have received us
>   by baptism into your Church:
>   we bless you for your Spirit ever within us,
>   your fatherly care to guide us and make us holy,
>   and for the enrichment of your grace.
>
>   Praise the Lord.
>   **Thanks be to God.**
>
>   The grace of the Lord Jesus Christ, the love of God, and
>   the fellowship of the Holy Spirit, be with us all. **Amen.**

Alternative Service

The Day of Teaching

Today we remember that Jesus taught in the courts of
the temple, replied to the questions by which his enemies
sought to incriminate him, and spoke parables of
judgement and salvation.

SENTENCE

Jesus said: I have not spoken on my own authority; the
Father who sent me has himself given me commandment
what to say and what to speak.

HYMN

PRAYER

Almighty and everlasting God,
who in your tender love towards mankind
    sent your Son our Saviour Jesus Christ
to take upon him our flesh
and to suffer death upon the cross:
grant that we may follow the example
    of his patience and humility,
and also be made partakers of his resurrection;
through Jesus Christ our Lord. **Amen.**

or

Almighty God,
whose most dear Son went not up to joy
    but first he suffered pain,
and entered not into glory before he was crucified;
mercifully grant that we, walking in the way of the cross,
may find it none other than the way of life and peace;
through Jesus Christ your Son our Lord,
who is alive and reigns with you and the Holy Spirit,
one God, for ever and ever. **Amen.**

5   OLD TESTAMENT

Isaiah 42.1–7

Behold my servant, whom I uphold,
    my chosen, in whom my soul delights;
I have put my Spirit upon him,
    he will bring forth justice to the nations.
He will not cry or lift up his voice,
    or make it heard in the street;
a bruised reed he will not break,
    and a dimly burning wick he will not quench;
    he will faithfully bring forth justice.
He will not fail or be discouraged
    till he has established justice in the earth;
    and the coastlands wait for his law.
Thus says God, the Lord,
    who created the heavens and stretched them out,
    who spread forth the earth and what comes from it,
who gives breath to the people upon it
    and spirit to those who walk in it:
'I am the Lord, I have called you in righteousness,
    I have taken you by the hand and kept you;
I have given you as a covenant to the people,
    a light to the nations,
    to open the eyes that are blind,
to bring out the prisoners from the dungeon,
    from the prison those who sit in darkness.'

or *Isaiah 49.1–6*

Listen to me, O coastlands,
    and hearken, you peoples from afar.
The Lord called me from the womb,
    from the body of my mother he named my name.
He made my mouth like a sharp sword,
    in the shadow of his hand he hid me;
he made me a polished arrow,
    in his quiver he hid me away.

And he said to me, 'You are my servant,
   Israel, in whom I will be glorified.'
But I said, 'I have laboured in vain,
   I have spent my strength for nothing and vanity;
yet surely my right is with the Lord,
   and my recompense with my God.'
And now the Lord says,
   who formed me from the womb to be his servant,
to bring Jacob back to him,
   and that Israel might be gathered to him,
for I am honoured in the eyes of the Lord,
   and my God has become my strength –
he says:
'It is too light a thing that you should be my servant
   to raise up the tribes of Jacob
   and to restore the preserved of Israel;
I will give you as a light to the nations,
   that my salvation may reach to the end of the earth.'

6   The following psalm, or a hymn.

Psalm 56

1 Be merciful to me, O God, for men are treading me down:
    all day long my adversary presses upon me.

2 My enemies tread me down all the day:
    for there are many that arrogantly fight against me.

3 In the hour of fear:
    I will put my trust in you.

4 In God, whose word I praise, in God I trust and fear not:
    what can flesh do to me?

5 All day long they afflict me with their words:
    and every thought is how to do me evil.

6 They stir up hatred and conceal themselves:
    they watch my steps, while they lie in wait for my life.

7 Let there be no escape for them:
  bring down the peoples in your wrath, O God.

8 You have counted my anxious tossings;
      put my tears in your bottle:
  are not these things noted in your book?

9 In the day that I call to you, my enemies shall turn back:
  this I know, for God is with me.

10 In God, whose word I praise, in God I trust and fear not:
  what can man do to me?

11 To you, O God, must I perform my vows:
  I will pay the thank-offering that is due.

12 For you will deliver my soul from death,
      and my feet from falling:
  that I may walk before God in the light of the living.

7 GOSPEL

Mark 11.27—13.2

Jesus and the disciples came again to Jerusalem. And as Jesus
was walking in the temple, the chief priests and the scribes
and the elders came to him, and they said to him, 'By what
authority are you doing these things, or who gave you this
authority to do them?' Jesus said to them, 'I will ask you a
question; answer me, and I will tell you by what authority I do
these things. Was the baptism of John from heaven or from
men? Answer me.' And they argued with one another, 'If we
say, "From heaven," he will say, "Why then did you not
believe him?" But shall we say, "From men"?' – they were
afraid of the people, for all held that John was a real prophet.
So they answered Jesus, 'We do not know.' And Jesus said to
them, 'Neither will I tell you by what authority I do these
things.'

And he began to speak to them in parables. 'A man planted a vineyard, and set a hedge around it, and dug a pit for the wine press, and built a tower, and let it out to tenants, and went into another country. When the time came, he sent a servant to the tenants, to get from them some of the fruit of the vineyard. And they took him and beat him, and sent him away empty-handed. Again he sent to them another servant, and they wounded him in the head, and treated him shamefully. And he sent another, and him they killed; and so with many others, some they beat and some they killed. He had still one other, a beloved son; finally he sent him to them, saying, "They will respect my son." But those tenants said to one another, "This is the heir; come, let us kill him, and the inheritance will be ours." And they took him and killed him, and cast him out of the vineyard. What will the owner of the vineyard do? He will come and destroy the tenants, and give the vineyard to others. Have you not read this scripture:

"The very stone which the builders rejected
has become the head of the corner;
this was the Lord's doing,
and it is marvellous in our eyes"?'

And they tried to arrest him, but feared the multitude, for they perceived that he had told the parable against them; so they left him and went away.

And they sent to him some of the Pharisees and some of the Herodians, to entrap him in his talk. And they came and said to him, 'Teacher, we know that you are true, and care for no man; for you do not regard the position of men, but truly teach the way of God. Is it lawful to pay taxes to Caesar, or not? Should we pay them, or should we not?' But knowing their hypocrisy, he said to them, 'Why put me to the test? Bring me a coin, and let me look at it.' And they brought one. And he said to them, 'Whose likeness and inscription is this?' They said to him, 'Caesar's.' Jesus said to them, 'Render to Caesar the things that are Caesar's, and to God the things that are God's.' And they were amazed at him.

And Sadducees came to him, who say that there is no
resurrection; and they asked him a question, saying, 'Teacher,
Moses wrote for us that if a man's brother dies and leaves a
wife, but leaves no child, the man must take the wife, and
raise up children for his brother. There were seven brothers;
the first took a wife, and when he died he left no children; and
the second took her, and died, leaving no children; and the
third likewise; and the seven left no children. Last of all the
woman also died. In the resurrection whose wife will she be?
For the seven had her as wife.'

Jesus said to them, 'Is not this why you are wrong, that you
know neither the scriptures nor the power of God? For when
they rise from the dead, they neither marry nor are given in
marriage, but are like angels in heaven. And as for the dead
being raised, have you not read in the book of Moses, in the
passage about the bush, how God said to him, "I am the God
of Abraham, and the God of Isaac, and the God of Jacob"? He
is not God of the dead, but of the living; you are quite wrong.'

And one of the scribes came up and heard them disputing with
one another, and seeing that he answered them well, asked
him, 'Which commandment is the first of all?' Jesus answered,
'The first is, "Hear, O Israel: The Lord our God, the Lord is one;
and you shall love the Lord your God with all your heart, and
with all your soul, and with all your mind, and with all your
strength." The second is this, "You shall love your neighbour
as yourself." There is no other commandment greater than
these.' And the scribe said to him, 'You are right, Teacher; you
have truly said that he is one, and there is no other but he;
and to love him with all the heart, and with all the
understanding, and with all the strength, and to love one's
neighbour as oneself, is much more than all whole burnt
offerings and sacrifices.' And when Jesus saw that he
answered wisely, he said to him, 'You are not far from the
kingdom of God.' And after that no one dared to ask him any
question.

And as Jesus taught in the temple, he said, 'How can the scribes say that the Christ is the son of David? David himself, inspired by the Holy Spirit, declared,

"The Lord said to my Lord,
Sit at my right hand,
till I put your enemies under your feet."

David himself calls him Lord; so how is he his son?' And the great throng heard him gladly.

And in his teaching he said, 'Beware of the scribes, who like to go about in long robes, and to have salutations in the market places and the best seats in the synagogues and the places of honour at feasts, who devour widows' houses and for a pretence make long prayers. They will receive the greater condemnation.'

And he sat down opposite the treasury, and watched the multitude putting money into the treasury. Many rich people put in large sums. And a poor widow came, and put in two copper coins, which make a penny. And he called his disciples to him, and said to them, 'Truly, I say to you, this poor widow has put in more than all those who are contributing to the treasury. For they all contributed out of their abundance; but she out of her poverty has put in everything she had, her whole living.'

And as he came out of the temple, one of his disciples said to him, 'Look, Teacher, what wonderful stones and what wonderful buildings!' And Jesus said to him, 'Do you see these great buildings? There will not be left here one stone upon another, that will not be thrown down.'

or *Luke 20.1—21.4*

One day, as Jesus was teaching the people in the temple and preaching the gospel, the chief priests and the scribes with the elders came up and said to him, 'Tell us by what authority you do these things, or who it is that gave you this authority.' He answered them, 'I also will ask you a question; now tell me,

Was the baptism of John from heaven or from men?' And they discussed it with one another, saying, 'If we say, "From heaven," he will say, "Why did you not believe him?" But if we say, "From men," all the people will stone us; for they are convinced that John was a prophet.' So they answered that they did not know whence it was. And Jesus said to them, 'Neither will I tell you by what authority I do these things.'

And he began to tell the people this parable: 'A man planted a vineyard, and let it out to tenants, and went into another country for a long while. When the time came, he sent a servant to the tenants, that they should give him some of the fruit of the vineyard; but the tenants beat him, and sent him away empty-handed. And he sent another servant; him also they beat and treated shamefully, and sent him away empty-handed. And he sent yet a third; this one they wounded and cast out. Then the owner of the vineyard said, "What shall I do? I will send my beloved son; it may be they will respect him." But when the tenants saw him, they said to themselves, "This is the heir; let us kill him, that the inheritance may be ours." And they cast him out of the vineyard and killed him. What then will the owner of the vineyard do to them? He will come and destroy those tenants, and give the vineyard to others.' When they heard this, they said, 'God forbid!' But he looked at them and said, 'What then is this that is written:

"The very stone which the builders rejected
has become the head of the corner"?

Every one who falls on that stone will be broken to pieces; but when it falls on any one it will crush him.'

The scribes and the chief priests tried to lay hands on him at that very hour, but they feared the people; for they perceived that he had told this parable against them. So they watched him, and sent spies, who pretended to be sincere, that they might take hold of what he said, so as to deliver him up to the authority and jurisdiction of the governor. They asked him, 'Teacher, we know that you speak and teach rightly, and show no partiality, but truly teach the way of God. Is it lawful for us to give tribute to Caesar, or not?' But he perceived their craftiness, and said to them, 'Show me a coin. Whose likeness and inscription has it?' They said, 'Caesar's.' He said to them, 'Then render to Caesar the things that are Caesar's, and to God the things that are God's.' And they were not able in the presence of the people to catch him by what he said; but marvelling at his answer they were silent.

There came to him some Sadducees, those who say that there is no resurrection, and they asked him a question, saying, 'Teacher, Moses wrote for us that if a man's brother dies, having a wife but no children, the man must take the wife and raise up children for his brother. Now there were seven brothers; the first took a wife, and died without children; and the second and the third took her, and likewise all seven left no children and died. Afterward the woman also died. In the resurrection, therefore, whose wife will the woman be? For the seven had her as wife?'

And Jesus said to them, 'The sons of this age marry and are given in marriage; but those who are accounted worthy to attain to that age and to the resurrection from the dead neither marry nor are given in marriage, for they cannot die any more, because they are equal to angels and are sons of God, being sons of the resurrection. But that the dead are raised, even Moses showed, in the passage about the bush, where he calls the Lord the God of Abraham and the God of Isaac and the God of Jacob. Now he is not God of the dead, but of the living; for all live to him.' And some of the scribes answered, 'Teacher, you have spoken well.' For they no longer dared to ask him any question.

But he said to them, 'How can they say that the Christ is David's son? For David himself says in the Book of Psalms,

"The Lord said to my Lord,
Sit at my right hand,
till I make your enemies a stool for your feet."

93

David thus calls him Lord; so how is he his son?'

And in the hearing of all the people he said to his disciples, 'Beware of the scribes, who like to go about in long robes, and love salutations in the market places and the best seats in the synagogues and the places of honour at feasts, who devour widows' houses and for a pretence make long prayers. They will receive the greater condemnation.'

He looked up and saw the rich putting their gifts into the treasury; and he saw a poor widow put in two copper coins. And he said, 'Truly I tell you, this poor widow has put in more than all of them; for they all contributed out of their abundance, but she out of her poverty put in all the living that she had.'

8   SERMON

9   THANKSGIVING

> Lord God, we praise you:
> you created the heavens and spread them out;
> you gave shape to the earth and what comes from it;
> you gave breath to its people and life to the
>   creatures that move in it;
> yet in our pride and greed
> we have not yielded to you the fruit of obedient
>   gratitude.
>
> But when we disobeyed your law and defied your
>   prophets,
> you loved the world so much
> that in the fullness of time you sent to us your
>   only Son Jesus Christ
> in whom you delight;
> he lived as one of us, yet without sin.
> To fulfil your purpose
> he gave himself up to rejection and death;
> and rising from death he destroyed death

and became the chief cornerstone of the new creation;
he sits at your right hand,
pleading our cause,
till all things are put into subjection under him.

And that we might live no longer for ourselves
but for him who died and rose for us,
you sent the Holy Spirit
to complete his work in the world.

In penitence and poverty, Father,
we would give to you
all that we have and all that we are.
Grant to us, we pray, the strengthening power
    of the Holy Spirit
that following the teaching of our Lord Jesus Christ,
we may love you with all our heart and mind
    and soul and strength
and our neighbours as ourselves.

Make us a light to the nations,
that your salvation may reach to the ends of the earth.
This we ask through Jesus Christ
your Servant and our Saviour. **Amen.**

Or, if a Eucharist is to follow, this prayer may be said here:

Almighty God,
from your Son's parables of watchfulness
and coming judgement
help us to learn the grace of quiet faithfulness
and steady vigilance.
Grant that we may never tax his patience
nor provoke his wrath,
but with obedience and humility receive his truth
and feed upon it until our lives
become what you would have them be;
through Jesus Christ our Lord. **Amen.**

10 Intercession may follow here for

> those burdened by doubt;
> those whose faith is under strain;
> those who are preparing for baptism and confirmation;
> teachers and students of theology.

11 If there is no Eucharist, the service concludes with the Lord's
Prayer, a hymn and the dismissal.

WEDNESDAY

Service

1 SENTENCE

The Son of man did not come to be served, but to serve,
and to give up his life as a ransom for many.

2 HYMN

3 COLLECT

Almighty God,
whose Son Jesus Christ revealed your eternal glory
by taking the form of a servant:
set in our hearts his spirit of service,
that in sharing his humility and in serving one another
we may find our true greatness;
through Jesus Christ our Lord. **Amen.**

4 READINGS

Year 1	Year 2
Isaiah 50.4–9	*Numbers 21.4–9*
1 Peter 2.18–25	*1 Corinthians 1.18–25*
Mark 15.1–41	*Luke 23.1–47*

Psalms 102.1–11; 55.12–14

5 SERMON

6 The Creed may be said.

7 INTERCESSIONS

Eternal God, whose Son Jesus Christ, our servant Lord,
stands before us in the guise of the needy,
and calls to us in the cry of the distressed:
hear us as we pray for our brethren.

For the hungry, the refugees and the homeless;
For the poor, the diseased and the dying;
Lord, hear our prayer.

For the weak and the vulnerable;
For those who are easily overthrown by the stresses
of life;
Lord, hear our prayer.

For the incapacitated and the handicapped;
For the mentally afflicted and the depressed;
Lord, hear our prayer.

For the delinquent, the prisoner and the desperate;
For the alcoholic, the gambler and the drug addict;
Lord, hear our prayer.

For the aged, the lonely and the unloved;
For the fallen and those without hope;
Lord, hear our prayer.

For all agencies of relief and service
Lord, hear our prayer.

Help us, who offer these prayers, to take the sufferings of
others upon ourselves, and so, by your grace, become the
agents of your transforming love: through Jesus Christ
our Lord. **Amen.**

8   The following sentences are said and the gifts of the people are
received for those in need.

If a man has enough to live on, and yet when he sees his
brother in need shuts up his heart against him, how can
it be said that the divine love dwells in him?
This command comes to us from Christ himself: that he
who loves God must also love his brother.

9   THE PRAYER OVER THE GIFTS OF THE PEOPLE

Eternal God, receive our gifts and help us and all your people
to live and speak the good news of your love, that all human
life may be an offering to you: through Jesus Christ our Lord.
Amen.

10   The rest of the Eucharist now follows.

or

11   If there is no communion, the service ends with a prayer of
thanksgiving and the following:

The grace of the Lord Jesus Christ, the love of God, and
the fellowship of the Holy Spirit, be with us all. **Amen.**

Alternative Service

The Day of Waiting

1   Today we remember that while Judas was bargaining
with the authorities to betray his Master, a woman
anointed Jesus's head with precious ointment,
symbolically anticipating his coming death and burial.

2   SENTENCE

Jesus said: The hour has come for the Son of man to be
glorified. Now is my soul in turmoil. Shall I say 'Father,
save me from this hour?' No, it was for this that I came
to this hour. Father, glorify thy name.

3   HYMN

4   PRAYER

Almighty and everlasting God,
who in your tender love towards mankind
    sent your Son our Saviour Jesus Christ
to take upon him our flesh
and to suffer death upon the cross:
grant that we may follow the example
    of his patience and humility,
and also be made partakers of his resurrection;
through Jesus Christ our Lord. **Amen.**

or

Almighty God,
whose most dear Son went not up to joy
    but first he suffered pain,
and entered not into glory before he was crucified:
mercifully grant that we, walking in the way of the cross,
may find it none other than the way of life and peace;
through Jesus Christ your Son our Lord,

100   *Shorter edition page 47*

who is alive and reigns with you and the Holy Spirit,
one God, for ever and ever. **Amen.**

5 OLD TESTAMENT

Isaiah 50.4–9

The Lord God has given me
  the tongue of those who are taught,
that I may know how to sustain with a word
  him that is weary.
Morning by morning he wakens,
  he wakens my ear
  to hear as those who are taught.
The Lord God has opened my ear,
  and I was not rebellious,
  I turned not backward.
I gave my back to the smiters,
  and my cheeks to those who pulled out the beard;
I hid not my face
  from shame and spitting.
For the Lord God helps me;
  therefore I have not been confounded;
therefore I have set my face like a flint,
  and I know that I shall not be put to shame;
  he who vindicates me is near.
Who will contend with me?
  Let us stand up together.
Who is my adversary?
  Let him come near to me.
Behold, the Lord God helps me;
  who will declare me guilty?
Behold, all of them will wear out like a garment;
  the moth will eat them up.

or *Jeremiah 7.21–28*

Thus says the Lord of hosts, the God of Israel: 'Add your burnt
offerings to your sacrifices, and eat the flesh. For in the day

that I brought them out of the land of Egypt, I did not speak to
your fathers or command them concerning burnt offerings and
sacrifices. But this command I gave them, "Obey my voice,
and I will be your God, and you shall be my people; and walk
in all the way that I command you, that it may be well with
you." But they did not obey or incline their ear, but walked in
their own counsels and the stubbornness of their evil hearts,
and went backward and not forward. From the day that your
fathers came out of the land of Egypt to this day, I have
persistently sent all my servants the prophets to them, day
after day; yet they did not listen to me, or incline their ear, but
stiffened their neck. They did worse than their fathers.

'So you shall speak all these words to them, but they will not
listen to you. You shall call to them, but they will not answer
you. And you shall say to them, "This is the nation that did
not obey the voice of the Lord their God, and did not accept
discipline; truth has perished; it is cut off from their lips."'

6   The following psalm, or a hymn.

Psalm 40

1   I waited patiently for the Lord:
     and he inclined to me and heard my cry.

2   He brought me up from the pit of roaring waters,
         out of the mire and clay:
     and set my feet upon a rock, and made firm my foothold.

3   And he has put a new song in my mouth:
     even a song of thanksgiving to our God.

4   Many shall see it and fear:
     and shall put their trust in the Lord.

5   Blessed is the man who has made the Lord his hope:
     who has not turned to the proud,
         or to those who wander in deceit.

6 O Lord my God,
    great are the wonderful things which you have done,
    and your thoughts which are towards us:
there is none to be compared with you;

7 Were I to declare them and speak of them:
they are more than I am able to express.

8 Sacrifice and offering you do not desire:
but my ears you have marked for obedience;

9 Burnt-offering and sin-offering you have not required;
then said I, Lo, I come.

10 In the scroll of the book it is written of me,
    that I should do your will:
O my God, I long to do it, your law delights my heart.

11 I have declared your righteousness
    in the great congregation:
I have not restrained my lips, O Lord,
    and that you know.

12 I have not hidden your righteousness in my heart:
I have spoken of your faithfulness and of your salvation.

13 I have not kept back your loving-kindness and your truth:
from the great congregation.

14 O Lord, do not withhold your mercy from me:
let your loving-kindness and your truth ever preserve me.

15 For innumerable troubles have come upon me:
my sins have overtaken me, and I cannot see.

16 They are more in number than the hairs of my head:
therefore my heart fails me.

17 Be pleased, O Lord, to deliver me:
O Lord, make haste to help me.

18 Let those who seek my life to take it away:
be put to shame and confounded altogether.

19 Let them be turned back and disgraced who wish me evil:
    let them be aghast for shame who say to me 'Aha, aha!'

20 Let all who seek you be joyful and glad because of you:
    let those who love your salvation say always
        'The Lord is great.'

21 As for me, I am poor and needy:
    but the Lord will care for me.

22 You are my helper and my deliverer:
    make no long delay, O Lord my God.

7   GOSPEL

Mark 14.1–11

It was now two days before the Passover and the feast of
Unleavened Bread. And the chief priests and the scribes were
seeking how to arrest Jesus by stealth, and kill him; for they
said, 'Not during the feast, lest there be a tumult of the people.'

And while he was at Bethany in the house of Simon the leper,
as he sat at table, a woman came with an alabaster flask of
ointment of pure nard, very costly, and she broke the flask and
poured it over his head. But there were some who said to
themselves indignantly, 'Why was the ointment thus wasted?
For this ointment might have been sold for more than three
hundred denarii, and given to the poor.' And they reproached
her. But Jesus said, 'Let her alone; why do you trouble her?
She has done a beautiful thing to me. For you always have the
poor with you, and whenever you will, you can do good to
them; but you will not always have me. She has done what
she could; she has anointed my body beforehand for burying.
And truly, I say to you, wherever the gospel is preached in the
whole world, what she has done will be told in memory of her.'

Then Judas Iscariot, who was one of the twelve, went to the
chief priests in order to betray him to them. And when they
heard it they were glad, and promised to give him money. And
he sought an opportunity to betray him.

or *Matthew 26.3–16*

The chief priests and the elders of the people gathered in the palace of the high priest, who was called Caiaphas, and took counsel together in order to arrest Jesus by stealth and kill him. But they said, 'Not during the feast, lest there be a tumult among the people.'

Now when Jesus was at Bethany in the house of Simon the leper, a woman came up to him with an alabaster jar of very expensive ointment, and she poured it on his head, as he sat at table. But when the disciples saw it, they were indignant, saying, 'Why this waste? For this ointment might have been sold for a large sum, and given to the poor.' But Jesus, aware of this, said to them, 'Why do you trouble the woman? For she has done a beautiful thing to me. For you always have the poor with you, but you will not always have me. In pouring this ointment on my body she has done it to prepare me for burial. Truly, I say to you, wherever this gospel is preached in the whole world, what she has done will be told in memory of her.'

Then one of the twelve, who was called Judas Iscariot, went to the chief priests and said, 'What will you give me if I deliver him to you?' And they paid him thirty pieces of silver. And from that moment he sought an opportunity to betray him.

8   SERMON

9   THANKSGIVING

> Almighty God, Creator of the universe,
> glorious and good beyond our understanding,
> we praise you.
> You have given us life
> that we may pour it out as an offering
>   of love and service.

We have sinned against you
by resisting this your purpose
and wasting the gifts which you have given to us,
but you have sent your Son Jesus Christ,
who for us became as we are,
and met our poverty at his cost.
We thank you that for us he endured betrayal,
    mockery and death.
You raised him from the dead
and gave to him the Name that is above every name;
in majesty he ascended into heaven
where he intercedes for us as one who knows
    our weakness.

We thank you for the Holy Spirit
whom you have sent to bring us to new life in Christ
and the freedom to call you Father.

With the woman who anointed Christ
we offer to you our love and our devotion;
help us not to count the cost of service
nor to betray our high calling in Christ;
may we live not for ourselves
but for him who died for us.
Accept our offering, we pray,
not for our sake,
but for the sake of Jesus Christ our Saviour. **Amen.**

Or, if a Eucharist is to follow, this prayer may be said here:

Almighty God, as we remember your Son
seeking strength in you before his Passion,
we pray for your enabling grace to support us
    in all tensions and temptations.
From his example teach us the grace of acceptance
and in the power of his victory give us strength
to conquer all our fears and our weaknesses.
Grant that our lives be made an offering of true devotion
and save us from betraying our Lord in any way;
through Jesus Christ our Lord. **Amen.**

10 Intercession may follow here for

> those facing trials and hardships;
> those who are going through a time of temptation;
> all who seek, in different ways, to serve Christ.

11 If there is no Eucharist, the service concludes with the Lord's Prayer, a hymn and the dismissal.

MAUNDY THURSDAY

The Upper Room

1 INTRODUCTION

The minister may introduce the service in the following or similar words:

> Today we remember that our Lord washed his disciples' feet, and instituted the sacrament of his Body and Blood. He prayed that his disciples might be one, and gave them his peace and his New Commandment.

2 SENTENCE

> God shows his love for us in that while we were yet sinners Christ died for us.

3 HYMN

4 PRAYER

One of the following Collects is said:

> God our Father,
> we are gathered here to celebrate and share
> the supper which your only Son left to his Church:
> As we keep the feast of his redeeming love,
> may we feed on him by faith,
> receive his grace
> and find the fullness of love and life.
> This we pray through our Lord Jesus Christ. **Amen.**

or

Almighty and heavenly Father,
we thank you that in this wonderful sacrament
you have given us the memorial
    of the passion of your Son Jesus Christ.
Grant us so to reverence
the sacred mysteries of his Body and Blood,
that we may know within ourselves
and show forth in our lives
    the fruits of his redemption;
who is alive and reigns with you and the Holy Spirit,
one God, now and for ever. **Amen.**

5   OLD TESTAMENT

Year 1   *Exodus 12.1–8, 11–14*

The Lord said to Moses and Aaron in the land of Egypt, 'This
month shall be for you the beginning of months; it shall be the
first month of the year for you. Tell all the congregation of
Israel that on the tenth day of this month they shall take
every man a lamb according to their fathers' houses, a lamb
for a household; and if the household is too small for a lamb,
then a man and his neighbour next to his house shall take
according to the number of persons; according to what each
can eat you shall make your count for the lamb. Your lamb
shall be without blemish, a male a year old; you shall take it
from the sheep or from the goats; and you shall keep it until
the fourteenth day of this month, when the whole assembly of
the congregation of Israel shall kill their lambs in the evening.
Then they shall take some of the blood, and put it on the two
doorposts and the lintel of the houses in which they eat them.
They shall eat the flesh that night, roasted; with unleavened
bread and bitter herbs they shall eat it. In this manner you
shall eat it: your loins girded, your sandals on your feet, and
your staff in your hand; and you shall eat it in haste. It is the
Lord's passover. For I will pass through the land of Egypt that
night, and I will smite all the first-born in the land of Egypt,

both man and beast; and on all the gods of Egypt I will execute judgments: I am the Lord. The blood shall be a sign for you, upon the houses where you are; and when I see the blood, I will pass over you, and no plague shall fall upon you to destroy you, when I smite the land of Egypt.

This day shall be for you a memorial day, and you shall keep it as a feast to the Lord; throughout your generations you shall observe it as an ordinance for ever.'

Year 2   *Jeremiah 31.31–34*

'Behold, the days are coming, says the Lord, when I will make a new covenant with the house of Israel and the house of Judah, not like the covenant which I made with their fathers when I took them by the hand to bring them out of the land of Egypt, my covenant which they broke, though I was their husband, says the Lord. But this is the covenant which I will make with the house of Israel after those days, says the Lord: I will put my law within them, and I will write it upon their hearts; and I will be their God, and they shall be my people. And no longer shall each man teach his neighbour and each his brother, saying, "Know the Lord," for they shall all know me, from the least of them to the greatest, says the Lord; for I will forgive their iniquity, and I will remember their sin no more.'

The following psalm, or a hymn.

Psalm 116.11–18

V I will take up the cup of salvation and call upon the name of the Lord.
R **When we bless the cup of blessing it is a sharing in the Blood of Christ.**

All

11 How shall I repay the Lord:
    for all his benefits to me?

12 I will take up the cup of salvation:
      and call upon the name of the Lord.

13 I will pay my vows to the Lord:
      in the presence of all his people.

14 Grievous in the sight of the Lord:
      is the death of his faithful ones.

15 O Lord, I am your servant,
        your servant and the son of your handmaid:
      you have unloosed my bonds.

16 I will offer you a sacrifice of thanksgiving:
      and call upon the name of the Lord.

17 I will pay my vows to the Lord:
      in the presence of all his people,

18 In the courts of the house of the Lord:
      even in your midst, O Jerusalem. Praise the Lord.

V   I will take the cup of blessing and call upon the name of
      the Lord.
R   **When we bless the cup of blessing it is a sharing in the
      Blood of Christ.**

7   Here may be read the Epistle (see 15) if it is not to be read later.

8   GOSPEL

    Year 1   *John 13.1–15*

    Now before the feast of the Passover, when Jesus knew that
    his hour had come to depart out of this world to the Father,
    having loved his own who were in the world, he loved them to
    the end. And during supper, when the devil had already put it
    into the heart of Judas Iscariot, Simon's son, to betray him,
    Jesus, knowing that the Father had given all things into his
    hands, and that he had come from God and was going to God,
    rose from supper, laid aside his garments, and girded himself
    with a towel. Then he poured water into a basin, and began to

wash the disciples' feet, and to wipe them with the towel with which he was girded. He came to Simon Peter; and Peter said to him, 'Lord, do you wash my feet?' Jesus answered him, 'What I am doing you do not know now, but afterward you will understand.' Peter said to him, 'You shall never wash my feet.' Jesus answered him, 'If I do not wash you, you have no part in me.' Simon Peter said to him, 'Lord, not my feet only but also my hands and my head!' Jesus said to him, 'He who has bathed does not need to wash, except for his feet, but he is clean all over; and you are clean, but not all of you.' For he knew who was to betray him; that was why he said, 'You are not all clean.'

When he had washed their feet, and taken his garments, and resumed his place, he said to them, 'Do you know what I have done to you? You call me Teacher and Lord; and you are right, for so I am. If I then, your Lord and Teacher, have washed your feet, you also ought to wash one another's feet.'

Year 2   *Mark 14.12–26*

On the first day of Unleavened Bread, when they sacrificed the passover lamb, his disciples said to Jesus, 'Where will you have us go and prepare for you to eat the passover?' And he sent two of his disciples, and said to them, 'Go into the city, and a man carrying a jar of water will meet you, follow him, and wherever he enters, say to the householder, "The Teacher says, Where is my guest room, where I am to eat the passover with my disciples?" And he will show you a large upper room furnished and ready; there prepare for us.' And the disciples set out and went to the city, and found it as he had told them; and they prepared the passover.

And when it was evening he came with the twelve. And as they were at table eating, Jesus said, 'Truly, I say to you, one of you will betray me, one who is eating with me.' They began to be sorrowful, and to say to him one after another, 'Is it I?' He said to them, 'It is one of the twelve, one who is dipping bread in the same dish with me. For the son of man goes as it is written of him, but woe to that man by whom the Son of man is betrayed! It would have been better for that man if he had not been born.'

And as they were eating, he took bread, and blessed, and broke it, and gave it to them, and said, 'Take; this is my body.' And he took a cup, and when he had given thanks he gave it to them, and they all drank of it. And he said to them, 'This is my blood of the covenant, which is poured out for many. Truly, I say to you, I shall not drink again of the fruit of the vine until that day when I drink it new in the kingdom of God.'

And when they had sung a hymn, they went out to the Mount of Olives.

9   During the reading of the Gospel, following it, or at a later point in the service, the ceremony of the washing of the feet may take place.
The minister pours water over the feet of those who are invited to represent the disciples. He wipes their feet with a towel. If John 13.1–15 has not been read as the Gospel lesson, the following portion from John 13.5 and 13.34–35 is now read.

> Then Jesus poured water into a basin, and began to wash the disciples' feet and to wipe them with the towel with which he was girded. And he said, 'A new commandment I give to you, that you love one another; even as I have loved you, that you also love one another. By this all men will know that you are my disciples, if you have love for one another.'

0 PRAYER

> Almighty Father,
> whose Son Jesus Christ has taught us
> that what we do for the least of our brethren
>   we do also for him:
> give us the will to be the servant of others
>   as he was the servant of all,
> who gave up his life and died for us,
> yet is alive and reigns with you and the Holy Spirit,
> one God, now and for ever. **Amen.**

1 SERMON

2 THE COMMANDMENTS

> Our Lord Jesus Christ said, 'If you love me, keep my
> commandments; happy are those who hear the word
> God and keep it. You shall love the Lord your God with
> all your heart, with all your soul, with all your mind,
> and with all your strength. And you shall love your
> neighbour as yourself.'

> Jesus said, 'A new commandment I give to you, that you
> love one another, as I have loved you; so you are to love
> one another.'

3 HYMN   *Ubi Caritas*

God is love, and where true love is,
  God himself is there.

Here in Christ we gather, love of Christ our calling.
Christ, our love, is with us, gladness be his greeting.
Let us all revere and love him, God eternal.
Loving him, let each love Christ in all his people.

God is love, and where true love is,
  God himself is there.

When we Christians gather, members of one Body,
Let there be in us no discord, but one spirit.
Banished now be anger, strife and every quarrel.
Christ our God, be present always here among us.

God is love, and where true love is,
    God himself is there.

Grant us love's fulfilment, joy with all the blessed,
When we see your face, O Saviour, in its glory.
Shine on us, O purest Light of all creation,
Be our bliss while endless ages sing your praises.

God is love, and where true love is,
    God himself is there.

James Quinn, SJ (b. 1919), altered

A tune by Dom Gregory Murray to this translation can be found in *New Church Praise*; *Hymns for Celebration*; *More Hymns for Today*; *Hymns and Psalms*.

14 INTERCESSIONS

These should include prayers for

Christian unity and mission;
persecuted Christians;
the rejected and the unloved;
racial harmony;
the peace of the world.

They may conclude with the following:

If there is love among you, then all will know you are
my disciples.
May we be full of affection, kindly and humble-hearted.
How good and how lovely it is when we live together in
unity.
May we all be one that the world may believe. Amen.

15 The rest of the Eucharist now follows, including (if it has not
been used earlier in the service) the Epistle reading below, in
which case it should be read before the President takes the
bread and wine and before the Thanksgiving Prayer is said.

Year 1   1 *Corinthians* 11.23–29

For I received from the Lord what I also delivered to you, that the Lord Jesus on the night when he was betrayed took bread, and when he had given thanks, he broke it, and said, 'This is my body which is for you. Do this in remembrance of me.' In the same way also the cup, after supper, saying, 'This cup is the new covenant in my blood. Do this, as often as you drink it, in remembrance of me.' For as often as you eat this bread and drink the cup, you proclaim the Lord's death until he comes.

Whoever, therefore, eats the bread or drinks the cup of the Lord in an unworthy manner will be guilty of profaning the body and blood of the Lord. Let a man examine himself, and so eat of the bread and drink of the cup. For any one who eats and drinks without discerning the body eats and drinks judgment upon himself.

Year 2   1 *Corinthians* 10.16–17

The cup of blessing which we bless, is it not a participation in the blood of Christ? The bread which we break, is it not a participation in the body of Christ? Because there is one loaf, we who are many are one body, for we all partake of the same loaf.

16 THE CONCLUSION

The service ends with a hymn and this Dismissal.

> And when the disciples had sung a hymn they went out to the Mount of Olives. Christ became obedient unto death, even death on a cross. Go in peace.

17 All lights, except one, may be extinguished.

GOOD FRIDAY

The Cross

1 SENTENCE

> Christ the Lord became obedient unto death, even death
> on a cross.

2 HYMN

3 COLLECT

> Almighty Father,
> look with mercy on this your family
> for which our Lord Jesus Christ
>   was content to be betrayed
>   and given up into the hands of wicked men
>   and to suffer death upon the cross;
> who is alive and glorified
>   with you and the Holy Spirit,
> one God, now and for ever. **Amen.**

or some other prayer.

4 OLD TESTAMENT

Isaiah 52.13—53 end

Behold, my servant shall prosper,
    he shall be exalted and lifted up,
    and shall be very high.
As many were astonished at him –
    his appearance was so marred, beyond human semblance,
    and his form beyond that of the sons of men –
so shall he startle many nations;
    kings shall shut their mouths because of him;
for that which has not been told them they shall see,
    and that which they have not heard they shall understand.

Who has believed what we have heard?
    And to whom has the arm of the Lord been revealed?
For he grew up before him like a young plant,
    and like a root out of dry ground;
he had no form or comeliness that we should look at him,
    and no beauty that we should desire him.
He was despised and rejected by men;
    a man of sorrows, and acquainted with grief;
and as one from whom men hide their faces
    he was despised, and we esteemed him not.

Surely he has borne our griefs
    and carried our sorrows;
yet we esteemed him stricken,
    smitten by God, and afflicted.
But he was wounded for our transgressions,
    he was bruised for our iniquities;
upon him was the chastisement that made us whole,
    and with his stripes we are healed.
All we like sheep have gone astray;
    we have turned every one to his own way;
and the Lord has laid on him
    the iniquity of us all.

He was oppressed, and he was afflicted,
    yet he opened not his mouth;
like a lamb that is led to the slaughter,
    and like a sheep that before its shearers is dumb,
    so he opened not his mouth.
By oppression and judgment he was taken away;
    and as for his generation, who considered
that he was cut off out of the land of the living,
    stricken for the transgression of my people?
And they made his grave with the wicked
    and with a rich man in his death,
although he had done no violence,
    and there was no deceit in his mouth.

Yet it was the will of the Lord to bruise him;
   he has put him to grief;
when he makes himself an offering for sin,
   he shall see his offspring, he shall prolong his days;
the will of the Lord shall prosper in his hand;
   he shall see the fruit of the travail of his soul
      and be satisfied;
by his knowledge shall the righteous one, my servant,
   make many to be accounted righteous;
   and he shall bear their iniquities.
Therefore I will divide him a portion with the great,
   and he shall divide the spoil with the strong;
because he poured out his soul to death,
   and was numbered with the transgressors;
yet he bore the sin of many,
   and made intercession for the transgressors.

The following psalm, or a hymn.

Psalm 88.1–13

1 O Lord my God, I call for help by day:
    and by night also I cry out before you.

2 Let my prayer come into your presence:
    and turn your ear to my loud crying.

3 For my soul is filled with trouble:
    and my life has come even to the brink of the grave.

4 I am reckoned among those that go down to the Pit:
    I am a man that has no help.

5 I lie among the dead,
     like the slain that sleep in the grave:
   whom you remember no more,
     who are cut off from your power.

6 You have laid me in the lowest Pit:
    in darkness and in the watery depths.

7 Your wrath lies heavy upon me:
   and all your waves are brought against me.

8 You have put my friends far from me:
   and made me to be abhorred by them.

9 I am so fast in prison I cannot get free:
   my eyes fail because of my affliction.

10 Lord, I call to you every day:
   I stretch out my hands toward you.

11 Will you work wonders for the dead:
   or will the shades rise up again to praise you?

12 Shall your love be declared in the grave:
   or your faithfulness in the place of destruction?

13 Will your wonders be made known in the dark:
   or your righteousness
      in the land where all things are forgotten?

6   NEW TESTAMENT

Hebrews 10.11–25

Every priest stands daily at his service, offering repeatedly the
same sacrifices, which can never take away sins. But when
Christ had offered for all time a single sacrifice for sins, he sat
down at the right hand of God, then to wait until his enemies
should be made a stool for his feet. For by a single offering he
has perfected for all time those who are sanctified. And the
Holy Spirit also bears witness to us; for after saying,

'This is the covenant that I will make with them
after those days, says the Lord:
I will put my laws on their hearts,
and write them on their minds,'

then he adds,

'I will remember their sins and their misdeeds no more.'

Where there is forgiveness of these, there is no longer any offering for sin.

Therefore, brethren, since we have confidence to enter the sanctuary by the blood of Jesus, by the new and living way which he opened for us through the curtain, that is, through his flesh, and since we have a great priest over the house of God, let us draw near with a true heart in full assurance of faith, with our hearts sprinkled clean from an evil conscience and our bodies washed with pure water. Let us hold fast the confession of our hope without wavering, for he who promised is faithful; and let us consider how to stir up one another to love and good works, not neglecting to meet together, as is the habit of some, but encouraging one another, and all the more as you see the Day drawing near.

7   The following psalm, or a hymn.

Psalm 54

1 Save me, O God, by the power of your name:
  and vindicate me by your might.

2 Hear my prayer, O God:
  and listen to the words of my mouth.

3 For the insolent have risen against me:
  ruthless men, who have not set God before them,
    seek my life.

4 But surely God is my helper:
  the Lord is the upholder of my life.

[5 Let evil recoil on those that would waylay me:
  O destroy them in your faithfulness!]

6 Then will I offer you sacrifice with a willing heart:
  I will praise your name, O Lord, for it is good.

7 For you will deliver me from every trouble:
  my eyes shall see the downfall of my enemies.

8   GOSPEL

The Gospel may be read in a dramatic form (see p. 136)

John 18 and 19

Jesus went forth with his disciples across the Kidron valley,
where there was a garden, which he and his disciples entered.
Now Judas, who betrayed him, also knew the place; for Jesus
often met there with his disciples. So Judas, procuring a band
of soldiers and some officers from the chief priests and the
Pharisees, went there with lanterns and torches and weapons.
Then Jesus, knowing all that was to befall him, came forward
and said to them, 'Whom do you seek?' They answered him,
'Jesus of Nazareth.' Jesus said to them, 'I am he.' Judas, who
betrayed him, was standing with them. When he said to them,
'I am he,' they drew back and fell to the ground. Again he
asked them, 'Whom do you seek?' And they said, 'Jesus of
Nazareth.' Jesus answered, 'I told you that I am he; so, if you
seek me, let these men go.' This was to fulfil the word which
he had spoken, 'Of those whom you gave me I lost not one.'
Then Simon Peter, having a sword, drew it and struck the
high priest's slave and cut off his right ear. The slave's name
was Malchus. Jesus said to Peter, 'Put your sword into its
sheath; shall I not drink the cup which the Father has given
me?'

So the band of soldiers and their captain and the officers of the
Jews seized Jesus and bound him. First they led him to Annas;
for he was the father-in-law of Caiaphas, who was high priest
that year. It was Caiaphas who had given counsel to the Jews
that it was expedient that one man should die for the people.

Simon Peter followed Jesus, and so did another disciple. As
this disciple was known to the high priest, he entered the court
of the high priest along with Jesus, while Peter stood outside
at the door. So the other disciple, who was known to the high
priest, went out and spoke to the maid who kept the door, and
brought Peter in. The maid who kept the door said to Peter,
'Are not you also one of this man's disciples?' He said, 'I am

not.' Now the servants and officers had made a charcoal fire, because it was cold, and they were standing and warming themselves; Peter also was with them, standing and warming himself.

The high priest then questioned Jesus about his disciples and his teaching. Jesus answered him, 'I have spoken openly to the world; I have always taught in synagogues and in the temple, where all Jews come together; I have said nothing secretly. Why do you ask me? Ask those who have heard me, what I said to them; they know what I said.' When he had said this, one of the officers standing by struck Jesus with his hand, saying, 'Is that how you answer the high priest?' Jesus answered him, 'If I have spoken wrongly, bear witness to the wrong; but if I have spoken rightly, why do you strike me?' Annas then sent him bound to Caiaphas the high priest.

Now Simon Peter was standing and warming himself. They said to him, 'Are not you also one of his disciples?' He denied it and said, 'I am not.' One of the servants of the high priest, a kinsman of the man whose ear Peter had cut off, asked, 'Did I not see you in the garden with him?' Peter again denied it; and at once the cock crowed.

Then they led Jesus from the house of Caiaphas to the praetorium. It was early. They themselves did not enter the praetorium, so that they might not be defiled, but might eat the passover. So Pilate went out to them and said, 'What accusation do you bring against this man?' They answered him, 'If this man were not an evildoer, we would not have handed him over.' Pilate said to them, 'Take him yourselves and judge him by your own law.' The Jews said to him, 'It is not lawful for us to put any man to death.' This was to fulfil the word which Jesus had spoken to show by what death he was to die.

Pilate entered the praetorium again and called Jesus, and said to him, 'Are you the King of the Jews?' Jesus answered, 'Do you say this of your own accord, or did others say it to you about me?' Pilate answered, 'Am I a Jew? Your own nation and the chief priests have handed you over to me; what have you done?' Jesus answered, 'My kingship is not of this world; if my kingship were of this world, my servants would fight, that I might not be handed over to the Jews; but my kingship is not from the world.' Pilate said to him, 'So you are a king?' Jesus answered, 'You say that I am a king. For this I was born, and for this I have come into the world, to bear witness to the truth. Every one who is of the truth hears my voice.' Pilate said to him, 'What is truth?'

After he had said this, he went out to the Jews again, and told them, 'I find no crime in him. But you have a custom that I should release one man for you at the Passover; will you have me release for you the King of the Jews?' They cried out again, 'Not this man, but Barabbas!' Now Barabbas was a robber.

Then Pilate took Jesus and scourged him. And the soldiers plaited a crown of thorns, and put it on his head, and arrayed him in a purple robe; they came up to him, saying, 'Hail, King of the Jews!' and struck him with their hands. Pilate went out again, and said to them, 'See, I am bringing him out to you, that you may know that I find no crime in him.' So Jesus came out, wearing the crown of thorns and the purple robe. Pilate said to them, 'Behold the man!' When the chief priests and the officers saw him, they cried out, 'Crucify him, crucify him!' Pilate said to them, 'Take him yourselves and crucify him, for I find no crime in him.' The Jews answered him, 'We have a law, and by that law he ought to die, because he has made himself the Son of God.' When Pilate heard these words, he was the more afraid; he entered the praetorium again and said to Jesus, 'Where are you from?' But Jesus gave no answer. Pilate therefore said to him, 'You will not speak to me? Do you not know that I have power to release you, and power to crucify you?' Jesus answered him, 'You would have no power over me unless it had been given you from above; therefore he who delivered me to you has the greater sin.'

Upon this Pilate sought to release him, but the Jews cried out, 'If you release this man, you are not Caesar's friend; every one who makes himself a king sets himself against Caesar.' When Pilate heard these words, he brought Jesus out and sat down on the judgment seat at a place called The Pavement, and in Hebrew, Gabbatha. Now it was the day of Preparation of the Passover; it was about the sixth hour. He said to the Jews, 'Behold your King!' They cried out, 'Away with him, away with him, crucify him!' Pilate said to them, 'Shall I crucify your King?' The chief priests answered, 'We have no king but Caesar.' Then he handed him over to them to be crucified.

So they took Jesus, and he went out, bearing his own cross, to the place called the place of a skull, which is called in Hebrew Golgotha. There they crucified him, and with him two others, one on either side, and Jesus between them. Pilate also wrote a title and put it on the cross; it read, 'Jesus of Nazareth, the King of the Jews.' Many of the Jews read this title, for the place where Jesus was crucified was near the city; and it was written in Hebrew, in Latin, and in Greek. The chief priests of the Jews then said to Pilate, do not write, 'The King of the Jews', but, 'This man said, "I am King of the Jews."' Pilate answered, 'What I have written I have written.'

When the soldiers had crucified Jesus they took his garments and made four parts, one for each soldier; also his tunic. But the tunic was without seam, woven from top to bottom; so they said to one another, 'Let us not tear it, but cast lots for it to see whose it shall be.' This was to fulfil the scripture

'They parted my garments among them,
and for my clothing they cast lots.'

So the soldiers did this. But standing by the cross of Jesus were his mother, and his mother's sister, Mary the wife of Clopas, and Mary Magdalene. When Jesus saw his mother, and the disciple whom he loved standing near, he said to his mother, 'Woman, behold, your son!' Then he said to the disciple, 'Behold, your mother!' And from that hour the disciple took her to his own home.

After this Jesus, knowing that all was now finished, said (to fulfil the scripture), 'I thirst.' A bowl full of vinegar stood there; so they put a sponge full of the vinegar on hyssop and held it to his mouth. When Jesus had received the vinegar, he said, 'It is finished'; and he bowed his head and gave up his spirit.

Since it was the day of Preparation, in order to prevent the bodies from remaining on the cross on the sabbath (for that sabbath was a high day), the Jews asked Pilate that their legs might be broken, and that they might be taken away. So the soldiers came and broke the legs of the first, and of the other who had been crucified with him; but when they came to Jesus and saw that he was already dead, they did not break his legs. But one of the soldiers pierced his side with a spear, and at once there came out blood and water. He who saw it has borne witness – his testimony is true, and he knows that he tells the truth – that you also may believe. For these things took place that the scripture might be fulfilled, 'Not a bone of him shall be broken.' And again another scripture says, 'They shall look on him whom they have pierced.'

After this Joseph of Arimathea, who was a disciple of Jesus, but secretly, for fear of the Jews, asked Pilate that he might take away the body of Jesus, and Pilate gave him leave. So he came and took away his body. Nicodemus also, who had at first come to him by night, came bringing a mixture of myrrh and aloes, about a hundred pounds' weight. They took the body of Jesus, and bound it in linen cloths with the spices, as is the burial custom of the Jews. Now in the place where he was crucified there was a garden, and in the garden a new tomb where no one had ever been laid. So because of the Jewish day of Preparation, as the tomb was close at hand, they laid Jesus there.

9   SERMON

10   A hymn may be sung.

11 INTERCESSIONS

Let us pray for the Church.

Almighty and eternal God, your Spirit guides the Church
and makes it holy. Listen to our prayers and help us all
in our various vocations to do your work more faithfully.
We ask this through Christ our Lord. **Amen.**

Let us pray for the Jewish people.

Almighty and eternal God, long ago you gave your
promise to Abraham and his descendants. Listen to your
Church as we pray that the people you first made your
own may arrive at the fullness of redemption.
We ask this through Christ our Lord. **Amen.**

Let us pray for those who do not believe in Christ.

Almighty and eternal God, we pray for those who do not
acknowledge Christ, yet walk before you in sincerity of
heart. Grant that they may find the truth in him. Help
us all to grow in love, to grasp more fully the mystery of
your Godhead, and to become more perfect witnesses
to the world.
We ask this through Christ our Lord. **Amen.**

Let us pray for those who do not believe in God.

Almighty and eternal God, you created the human race
so that all might long to find you and have peace when
you are found. Grant that, in spite of the hurtful things
that stand in their way, those who do not believe may
recognize in the lives of Christians the tokens of your
love and mercy, and gladly acknowledge you as the one
true God and Father of us all.
We ask this through Christ our Lord. **Amen.**

Let us pray for all in public office.

Almighty and eternal God, the longings and rights of the peoples of the world are known to you. In your goodness watch over those in authority, that the whole human family may enjoy freedom, security and peace.
We ask this through Christ our Lord. **Amen.**

Let us pray for those in special need.

Almighty, everliving God, you give strength to the weary and new courage to those who have lost heart. Hear the prayers of all who call on you in any trouble, that they may have the joy of receiving your help in their need.
We ask this through Christ our Lord. **Amen.**

12 A cross may now be brought in and set before the people.

13 The Reproaches may now be said or sung.

> *My people, what have I done to you?*
> *How have I offended you? Answer me!*

> I led you out of Egypt, from slavery to freedom,
> but you led your Saviour to the cross.

> *My people, what have I done to you?*
> *How have I offended you? Answer me!*

> *Holy is God! Holy and strong!*
> *Holy immortal One, have mercy on us.*

> For forty years I led you safely through the desert.
> I fed you with manna from heaven,
> and brought you to a land of plenty;
> but you led your Saviour to the cross.

> *Holy is God! Holy and strong!*
> *Holy immortal One, have mercy on us.*

What more could I have done for you?
I planted you as my fairest vine,
But you yielded only bitterness:
When I was thirsty you gave me vinegar to drink,
and you pierced your Saviour's side with a lance.

Holy is God! Holy and strong!
Holy immortal One, have mercy on us.

I opened the sea before you,
but you opened my side with a spear.

My people, what have I done to you?
How have I offended you? Answer me!

I led you on your way in a pillar of cloud,
but you led me to Pilate's court.

My people, what have I done to you?
How have I offended you? Answer me!

I bore you up with manna in the desert,
but you struck me down and scourged me.

My people, what have I done to you?
How have I offended you? Answer me!

I gave you saving water from the rock,
but you gave me gall and vinegar to drink.

My people, what have I done to you?
How have I offended you? Answer me!

I gave you a royal sceptre,
but you gave me a crown of thorns.

My people, what have I done to you?
How have I offended you? Answer me!

I raised you to the height of majesty,
but you have raised me high on a cross.

My people, what have I done to you?
How have I offended you? Answer me!

V We praise and adore you, O Christ.
R **By your cross and precious blood you have redeemed us.**

V Worthy is the Lamb, the Lamb that was slain, to receive
all power and wealth, wisdom and might, honour and
glory and praise!
R **We praise and adore you, O Christ.**
By your cross and precious blood you have redeemed us.

V You are worthy, O Christ, for you were slain, and by
your blood you purchased for God men of every tribe and
language, people and nation; you have made them a
royal house, to serve our God as priests; and they shall
reign upon earth.
R **We praise and adore you, O Christ.**
By your cross and precious blood you have redeemed us.

V To him who loves us and has freed us from our sins by
his blood, and made us a kingdom, priests to his God and
Father.
R **To him be glory and dominion for ever and ever. Amen.**

14 This or some other hymn.

1 Sing, my tongue, the glorious battle,
Sing the ending of the fray;
Now above the Cross, the trophy,
Sound the loud triumphant lay:
Tell how Christ, the world's Redeemer,
As a Victim won the day.

2 God in pity saw man fallen,
Shamed and sunk in misery,
When he fell on death by tasting
Fruit of the forbidden tree;
Then another tree was chosen
Which the world from death should free.

3 Thus the scheme of our salvation
   Was of old in order laid,
   That the manifold deceiver's
   Art by art might be outweighed,
   And the lure the foe put forward
   Into means of healing made.

4 Therefore when the appointed fullness
   Of the holy time was come,
   He was sent who maketh all things
   Forth from God's eternal home;
   Thus he came to earth, incarnate,
   Offspring of a maiden's womb.

5 Thirty years among us dwelling,
   His appointed time fulfilled,
   Born for this, he meets his Passion,
   For that this he freely willed.
   On the Cross the Lamb is lifted
   Where his life-blood shall be spilled.

6 He endured the nails, the spitting,
   Vinegar, and spear, and reed;
   From that holy Body broken
   Blood and water forth proceed:
   Earth, and stars, and sky, and ocean
   By that flood from stain are freed.

7 Faithful Cross! above all other,
   One and only noble tree!
   None in foliage, none in blossom,
   None in fruit thy peer may be;
   Sweetest wood and sweetest iron!
   Sweetest weight is hung on thee.

8 Bend thy boughs, O Tree of Glory!
   Thy relaxing sinews bend;
   For awhile the ancient rigour
   That thy birth bestowed, suspend;
   And the King of heavenly beauty
   On thy bosom gently tend!

9   Thou alone wast counted worthy
    This world's ransom to uphold;
    For a shipwrecked race preparing
    Harbour, like the Ark of old;
    With the sacred Blood anointed
    From the smitten Lamb that rolled.

10 To the Trinity be glory
    Everlasting, as is meet;
    Equal to the Father, equal
    To the Son, and Paraclete:
    Trinal Unity, whose praises
    All created things repeat. **Amen.**

15 CLOSING PRAYERS

Almighty God,
whose most dear Son went not up to joy
    but first he suffered pain,
and entered not into glory before he was crucified:
mercifully grant that we, walking in the way of the cross,
may find it none other than the way of life and peace;
through Jesus Christ your Son our Lord,
who is alive and reigns with you and the Holy Spirit,
one God, for ever and ever. **Amen.**

Lord Jesus Christ, Son of the living God,
we pray you to set your passion, cross and death
between your judgement and our souls,
now and in the hour of our death.
Give mercy and grace to the living;
pardon and rest to the dead;
to your holy Church peace and concord,
and to us sinners everlasting life and glory;
for with the Father and Holy Spirit
    you are alive and reign,
one God, now and for ever. **Amen.**

Living God,
at the evening hour your Son our Lord Jesus Christ
    lay in the tomb
and so hallowed the grave to be a bed of hope
    to all who put their trust in you:
give us such sorrow for our sins,
which were the cause of his passion,
that, when our bodies lie in the dust,
our souls may live with him;
for he is now alive and reigns with you
    and the Holy Spirit,
one God, now and for ever. **Amen.**

Jesus, Saviour of the world, come to us in your mercy:
we look to you to save and help us.

By your cross and your life laid down you set your
    people free:
we look to you to save and help us.

When they were ready to perish you saved your
    disciples:
we look to you to come to our help.

In the greatness of your mercy loose us from our chains:
forgive the sins of all your people.

Make yourself known as our Saviour and mighty
    Deliverer:
save and help us that we may praise you.

Come now and dwell with us, Lord Christ Jesus:
hear our prayer and be with us always.

And when you come in your glory:
**make us to be one with you and to share the life of
    your kingdom.**

If there is to be a communion, it may follow 11 or 14, and the
closing prayers may then be omitted.

The Passion of Our Lord Jesus Christ according to John   *John 18 and 19*

N   Jesus went forth with his disciples across the Kidron valley, where there was a garden, which he and his disciples entered. Now Judas, who betrayed him, also knew the place; for Jesus often met there with his disciples. So Judas, procuring a band of soldiers and some officers from the chief priests and the Pharisees, went there with lanterns and torches and weapons. Then Jesus, knowing all that was to befall him, came forward and said to them,

✠   Whom do you seek?

N   They answered him,

C   Jesus of Nazareth.

N   Jesus said to them,

✠   I am he.

N   Judas, who betrayed him, was standing with them. When he said to them, 'I am he,' they drew back and fell to the ground. Again he asked them,

✠   Whom do you seek?

N   And they said,

C   Jesus of Nazareth.

N   Jesus answered,

✠   I told you that I am he; so, if you seek me, let these men go.

N   This was to fulfil the word which he had spoken, 'Of those whom thou gavest me I lost not one.' Then Simon Peter, having a sword, drew it and struck the high priest's slave and cut off his right ear. The slave's name was Malchus. Jesus said to Peter,

✠   Put your sword into its sheath; shall I not drink the cup which the Father has given me?

N   So the band of soldiers and their captain and the officers
      of the Jews seized Jesus and bound him. First they led
      him to Annas; for he was the father-in-law of Caiaphas,
      who was high priest that year. It was Caiaphas who had
      given counsel to the Jews that it was expedient that one
      man should die for the people.

      Simon Peter followed Jesus, and so did another disciple. As
      this disciple was known to the high priest, he entered the
      court of the high priest along with Jesus, while Peter stood
      outside at the door. So the other disciple, who was known
      to the high priest, went out and spoke to the maid who
      kept the door, and brought Peter in. The maid who kept
      the door said to Peter,

R   Are not you also one of this man's disciples?

N   He said,

R   I am not.

N   Now the servants and officers had made a charcoal fire,
      because it was cold, and they were standing and warming
      themselves; Peter also was with them, standing and
      warming himself.

      The high priest then questioned Jesus about his disciples
      and his teaching. Jesus answered him,

✠   I have spoken openly to the world; I have always taught in
      synagogues and in the temple, where all Jews come
      together; I have said nothing secretly. Why do you ask me?
      Ask those who have heard me, what I said to them; they
      know what I said.

N   When he had said this, one of the officers standing by
      struck Jesus with his hand, saying,

R   Is that how you answer the high priest?

N   Jesus answered him,

✠   If I have spoken wrongly, bear witness to the wrong; but if
      I have spoken rightly, why do you strike me?

N   Annas then sent him bound to Caiaphas the high priest.

Now Simon Peter was standing and warming himself. They said to him,

C   Are not you also one of his disciples?

N   He denied it and said,

R   I am not.

N   One of the servants of the high priest, a kinsman of the man whose ear Peter had cut off, asked,

R   Did I not see you in the garden with him?

N   Peter again denied it; and at once the cock crowed.

Then they led Jesus from the house of Caiaphas to the praetorium. It was early. They themselves did not enter the praetorium, so that they might not be defiled, but might eat the passover. So Pilate went out to them and said,

R   What accusation do you bring against this man?

N   They answered him,

C   If this man were not an evildoer, we would not have handed him over.

N   Pilate said to them,

R   Take him yourselves and judge him by your own law.

N   The Jews said to him,

C   It is not lawful for us to put any man to death.

N   This was to fulfil the word which Jesus had spoken to show by what death he was to die.

Pilate entered the praetorium again and called Jesus, and said to him,

R   Are you the King of the Jews?

N   Jesus answered,

✠   Do you say this of your own accord, or did others say it to you about me?

N   Pilate answered,

R   Am I a Jew? Your own nation and the chief priests have handed you over to me; what have you done?

N   Jesus answered,

✠   My kingship is not of this world; if my kingship were of this world, my servants would fight, that I might not be handed over to the Jews; but my kingship is not from the world.

N   Pilate said to him,

R   So you are a king?

N   Jesus answered,

✠   You say that I am a king. For this I was born, and for this I have come into the world, to bear witness to the truth. Every one who is of the truth hears my voice.

N   Pilate said to him,

R   What is truth?

N   After he had said this, he went out to the Jews again, and told them,

R   I find no crime in him. But you have a custom that I should release one man for you at the Passover; will you have me release for you the King of the Jews?

N   They cried out again,

C   Not this man, but Barabbas!

N   Now Barabbas was a robber.

Then Pilate took Jesus and scourged him. And the soldiers plaited a crown of thorns, and put it on his head, and arrayed him in a purple robe; they came up to him, saying,

C   Hail, King of the Jews!

N   and struck him with their hands. Pilate went out again, and said to them,

R   See, I am bringing him out to you, that you may know that I find no crime in him.

N   So Jesus came out, wearing the crown of thorns and the purple robe. Pilate said to them,

R   Behold the man!

N   When the chief priests and the officers saw him, they cried out,

C   Crucify him, crucify him!

N   Pilate said to them,

R   Take him yourselves and crucify him, for I find no crime in him.

N   The Jews answered him,

C   We have a law, and by that law he ought to die, because he has made himself the Son of God.

N   When Pilate heard these words, he was the more afraid; he entered the praetorium again and said to Jesus,

R   Where are you from?

N   But Jesus gave no answer. Pilate therefore said to him,

R   You will not speak to me? Do you not know that I have power to release you, and power to crucify you?

N   Jesus answered him,

✠   You would have no power over me unless it had been given you from above; therefore he who delivered me to you has the greater sin.

N　Upon this Pilate sought to release him, but the Jews cried out,

C　If you release this man, you are not Caesar's friend; every one who makes himself a king sets himself against Caesar.

N　When Pilate heard these words, he brought Jesus out and sat down on the judgment seat at a place called The Pavement, and in Hebrew, Gabbatha. Now it was the day of Preparation of the Passover; it was about the sixth hour. He said to the Jews,

R　Behold your King!

N　They cried out,

C　Away with him, away with him, crucify him!

N　Pilate said to them,

R　Shall I crucify your King?

N　The chief priests answered,

C　We have no king but Caesar.

N　Then he handed him over to them to be crucified.

So they took Jesus, and he went out, bearing his own cross, to the place called the place of a skull, which is called in Hebrew Golgotha. There they crucified him, and with him two others, one on either side, and Jesus between them. Pilate also wrote a title and put it on the cross; it read, 'Jesus of Nazareth, the King of the Jews.' Many of the Jews read this title, for the place where Jesus was crucified was near the city; and it was written in Hebrew, in Latin, and in Greek. The chief priests of the Jews then said to Pilate,

C　Do not write, 'The King of the Jews,' but, 'This man said, "I am King of the Jews." '

N　Pilate answered,

R　What I have written I have written.

N   When the soldiers had crucified Jesus they took his
       garments and made four parts, one for each soldier; also
       his tunic. But the tunic was without seam, woven from top
       to bottom; so they said to one another,

C   Let us not tear it, but cast lots for it to see whose it shall be.

N   This was to fulfil the scripture,
       'They parted my garments among them,
       and for my clothing they cast lots.'

       So the soldiers did this. But standing by the cross of Jesus
       were his mother, and his mother's sister, Mary the wife of
       Clopas, and Mary Magdalene. When Jesus saw his mother,
       and the disciple whom he loved standing near, he said to
       his mother,

✠   Woman, behold, your son!

N   Then he said to the disciple,

✠   Behold, your mother!

N   And from that hour the disciple took her to his own home.

N   After this Jesus, knowing that all was now finished, said
       (to fulfil the scripture),

✠   I thirst.

N   A bowl full of vinegar stood there; so they put a sponge full
       of the vinegar on hyssop and held it to his mouth. When
       Jesus had received the vinegar, he said,

✠   It is finished;

N   and he bowed his head and gave up his spirit.

       Since it was the day of Preparation, in order to prevent the
       bodies from remaining on the cross on the sabbath (for that
       sabbath was a high day), the Jews asked Pilate that their
       legs might be broken, and that they might be taken away.
       So the soldiers came and broke the legs of the first, and of
       the other who had been crucified with him; but when they

came to Jesus and saw that he was already dead, they did not break his legs. But one of the soldiers pierced his side with a spear, and at once there came out blood and water. He who saw it has borne witness – his testimony is true, and he knows that he tells the truth – that you also may believe. For these things took place that the scripture might be fulfilled, 'Not a bone of him shall be broken.' And again another scripture says, 'They shall look on him whom they have pierced.'

After this Joseph of Arimathea, who was a disciple of Jesus, but secretly, for fear of the Jews, asked Pilate that he might take away the body of Jesus, and Pilate gave him leave. So he came and took away his body. Nicodemus also, who had at first come to him by night, came bringing a mixture of myrrh and aloes, about a hundred pounds' weight. They took the body of Jesus, and bound it in linen cloths with the spices, as is the burial custom of the Jews. Now in the place where he was crucified there was a garden, and in the garden a new tomb where no one had ever been laid. So because of the Jewish day of Preparation, as the tomb was close at hand, they laid Jesus there.

THE EASTER VIGIL

This service may be held either after dark on the Eve of Easter or on the morning of Easter Day. The church shall if possible be in darkness, except for a light to enable the readers to see the Bible on the lectern.

THE PREPARATION

1 Before the service begins, the minister stands before the congregation and says the following or similar words:

> We have gathered together to await the risen Christ. We shall listen to readings of Scripture, some of which were formerly used to give instruction to those about to be baptized into the death and resurrection of our Lord. We shall affirm our baptism and then joyfully await the Lord's coming to us in the breaking of the bread. Let us then prepare for this service in silence.

The people sit for the readings and stand for the prayers.

THE READINGS

2 Minister

> Let us pray.
>
> Almighty God, from the beginning of time
> you have been working for the salvation of the world.
> By the strength of your right hand
> you rescued your people from their slavery in Egypt:
> By the same power
> set free all the peoples of the world
>   from the bondage of their sins
> and make them heirs of the glories
>   of your everlasting kingdom;
> through Jesus Christ our Lord. **Amen.**

3   Reader

> The first reading is from the first chapter of Genesis. In it
> we hear that God created the universe and everything in
> it. He made all things after their kind. He made man and
> woman, in his own image. All that he made was good.

Genesis 1.1–15, 26–28, 31

In the beginning God created the heavens and the earth. The
earth was without form and void, and darkness was upon the
face of the deep; and the Spirit of God was moving over the
face of the waters.

And God said, 'Let there be light'; and there was light. And
God saw that the light was good; and God separated the light
from the darkness. God called the light Day, and the darkness
he called Night. And there was evening and there was
morning, one day.

And God said, 'Let there be a firmament in the midst of the
waters, and let it separate the waters from the waters.' And
God made the firmament and separated the waters which
were under the firmament from the waters which were above
the firmament. And it was so. And God called the firmament
Heaven. And there was evening and there was morning, a
second day.

And God said, 'Let the waters under the heavens be gathered
together into one place, and let the dry land appear.' And it
was so. God called the dry land Earth, and the waters that
were gathered together he called Seas. And God saw that it
was good. And God said, 'Let the earth put forth vegetation,
plants yielding seed, and fruit trees bearing fruit in which is
their seed, each according to its kind, upon the earth.' And it
was so. The earth brought forth vegetation, plants yielding
seed according to their own kinds, and trees bearing fruit in
which is their seed, each according to its kind. And God saw
that it was good. And there was evening and there was
morning, a third day.

And God said, 'Let there be lights in the firmament of the heavens to separate the day from the night; and let them be for signs and for seasons and for days and years, and let them be lights in the firmament of the heavens to give light upon the earth.' And it was so.

Then God said, 'Let us make man in our image, after our likeness; and let them have dominion over the fish of the sea, and over the birds of the air, and over the cattle, and over all the earth, and over every creeping thing that creeps upon the earth.' So God created man in his own image, in the image of God he created him; male and female he created them. And God blessed them, and God said to them, 'Be fruitful and multiply, and fill the earth and subdue it; and have dominion over the fish of the sea and over the birds of the air and over every living thing that moves upon the earth.'

And God saw everything that he had made, and behold, it was very good. And there was evening and there was morning, a sixth day.

SILENCE

Minister

> Let us pray.
>
> Almighty God,
> who wonderfully created us in your image
> and even more wonderfully restored us
> through your Son Jesus Christ:
> May we share in the divinity of Christ
> who humbled himself to share in our humanity;
> who is alive and reigns with you and the Holy Spirit,
> one God, now and for ever. **Amen.**

5   Reader

> The second reading is from the Book of Exodus. In it we hear that the people of God were meant to be free, but had become slaves in Egypt. God demands their release, and the cry 'Let my people go' rings through the land.

Exodus 4.27—5.1

The Lord said to Aaron, 'Go into the wilderness to meet Moses.' So he went, and met him at the mountain of God and kissed him. And Moses told Aaron all the words of the Lord with which he had sent him, and all the signs which he had charged him to do. Then Moses and Aaron went and gathered together all the elders of the people of Israel. And Aaron spoke all the words which the Lord had spoken to Moses, and did the signs in the sight of the people. And the people believed; and when they heard that the Lord had visited the people of Israel and that he had seen their affliction, they bowed their heads and worshipped. Afterward Moses and Aaron went to Pharaoh and said, 'Thus says the Lord, the God of Israel, "Let my people go, that they may hold a feast to me in the wilderness."'

SILENCE

6   Minister

> Let us pray.
>
> Almighty God, only hope of the world,
>   your messengers have said that it is your will
>   to liberate your people.
> Help us so to receive your word,
>   that we may not despair,
> but trust always in him
>   whom you have sent to rescue us,
>   your Son, Jesus Christ, our Lord. **Amen.**

Reader

> In the third reading, from the Book of Exodus, we hear of the rescue of the Israelites during their flight from Egypt. The story foreshadows our own deliverance through the waters of baptism, by which we enter into the liberty of the children of God.

Exodus 14.21–31

Then Moses stretched out his hand over the sea; and the Lord drove the sea back by a strong east wind all night, and made the sea dry land, and the waters were divided. And the people of Israel went into the midst of the sea on dry ground, the waters being a wall to them on their right hand and on their left. The Egyptians pursued, and went in after them into the midst of the sea, all Pharaoh's horses, his chariots, and his horsemen. And in the morning watch the Lord in the pillar of fire and of cloud looked down upon the host of the Egyptians, and discomfited the host of the Egyptians, clogging their chariot wheels so that they drove heavily; and the Egyptians said, 'Let us flee from before Israel; for the Lord fights for them against the Egyptians.'

Then the Lord said to Moses, 'Stretch out your hand over the sea, that the water may come back upon the Egyptians, upon their chariots, and upon their horsemen.' So Moses stretched forth his hand over the sea, and the sea returned to its wonted flow when the morning appeared; and the Egyptians fled into it, and the Lord routed the Egyptians in the midst of the sea. The waters returned and covered the chariots and the horsemen and all the host of Pharaoh that had followed them into the sea; not so much as one of them remained. But the people of Israel walked on dry ground through the sea, the waters being a wall to them on their right hand and on their left.

149

Thus the Lord saved Israel that day from the hand of the Egyptians; and Israel saw the Egyptians dead upon the seashore. And Israel saw the great work which the Lord did against the Egyptians, and the people feared the Lord; and they believed in the Lord and in his servant Moses.

SILENCE

8   Minister

> Let us pray.
>
> Almighty God,
> you rescued your people Israel from slavery in Egypt
> and led them through the waters of the Red Sea
> to the promised land:
> So we pray you to deliver the whole human race
>   from the bondage of sin
> through the waters of baptism
> and bring us to your heavenly kingdom,
> through Jesus Christ our Lord. **Amen.**

9   Reader

> The fourth lesson is from St Paul's letter to the Romans. In the sixth chapter the apostle Paul teaches us that in baptism we are united with our Redeemer in his death and in his resurrection.

Romans 6.3–11

Do you not know that all of us who have been baptized into Christ Jesus were baptized into his death? We were buried therefore with him by baptism into death, so that as Christ was raised from the dead by the glory of the Father, we too might walk in newness of life.

For if we have been united with him in a death like his, we shall certainly be united with him in a resurrection like his. We know that our old self was crucified with him so that the sinful body might be destroyed, and we might no longer be enslaved to sin. For he who has died is freed from sin. But if we have died with Christ, we believe that we shall also live with him. For we know that Christ being raised from the dead will never die again; death no longer has dominion over him. The death he died he died to sin, once for all, but the life he lives he lives to God. So you also must consider yourselves dead to sin and alive to God in Christ Jesus.

SILENCE

10 Minister

Let us pray.

Grant, Lord,
that we who are baptized into the death of
    your Son our Saviour Jesus Christ
may continually put to death our evil desires
and be buried with him;
that through the grave and gate of death
we may pass to our joyful resurrection;
through his merits, who died and was buried
    and rose again for us,
your Son Jesus Christ our Lord. **Amen.**

11 Reader

A reading from the Gospel according to Matthew. Our risen Lord makes himself known to those who had witnessed his death, and this moves them to worship.

Matthew 28.1–10

Now after the sabbath, toward the dawn of the first day of the week, Mary Magdalene and the other Mary went to see the sepulchre. And behold, there was a great earthquake; for an angel of the Lord descended from heaven and came and rolled back the stone, and sat upon it. His appearance was like lightning, and his raiment white as snow. And for fear of him the guards trembled and became like dead men. But the angel said to the women, 'Do not be afraid; for I know that you seek Jesus who was crucified. He is not here; for he has risen, as he said. Come, see the place where he lay. Then go quickly and tell his disciples that he has risen from the dead, and behold, he is going before you to Galilee; there you will see him. Lo, I have told you.' So they departed quickly from the tomb with fear and great joy, and ran to tell his disciples. And behold, Jesus met them and said, 'Hail!' And they came up and took hold of his feet and worshipped him. Then Jesus said to them, 'Do not be afraid; go and tell my brethren to go to Galilee, and there they will see me.'

12 After this the reader says:

Here end the readings from Holy Scripture.

Thanks be to God.

SILENCE

13 Minister

Let us pray.

Living Lord,
on the first Easter Day you stood among your disciples
and said 'Peace be unto you'.
Come to us, we pray, in your risen power
and make us glad with your presence;
for the glory of your great name. **Amen.**

The minister and his assistants prepare for the lighting of the candle.

The Service of Light

14 The minister says the following or similar words:

In this part of the service, the light which represents
Jesus Christ, the one true light of the world, is spread
progressively through the church, first to those nearest
the candle and then to the whole congregation. So we
are reminded that all Christians have their part to play
in the Church's mission of carrying the light of Christ's
gospel into every part of the world.

15 Minister

Let us pray.

Almighty God,
you sent your Son to be the light of the world
and to bring to your people the radiance of your glory.
Set us aflame with the fire of your love,
that with pure hearts and minds
we may come to the feast of everlasting light;
through Jesus Christ our Lord. **Amen.**

16 The minister takes a taper and lights the candle, saying:

May the light of the glorious and risen Christ banish all
darkness from our hearts and minds.

17 Having lit the candle, he hands it to an assistant who raises it
and says, or sings:

The Light of Christ.

Thanks be to God.

18 The procession moves along the nave and then stops. The
versicle and response are repeated in a louder voice, and then
the candles of all those in the procession are lit.

19 The procession moves again towards the place of baptism and stops once more. The versicle and response are again recited, louder still, then the candles of the congregation are lit.

20 The candle is placed in its stand near the place of baptism.*

21 Now follows THE EASTER PROCLAMATION. This outburst of praise is said or sung by an assistant standing near the candle.

> Rejoice, heavenly powers! Sing, choirs of angels!
> Exult, all creation around God's throne!
> Jesus Christ, our King, is risen!
> Sound the trumpet of salvation!
>
> Rejoice, O earth, in shining splendour,
> radiant in the brightness of your King!
> Christ has conquered! Glory fills you!
> Darkness vanishes for ever!
>
> Rejoice, O Mother Church! Exult in glory!
> The risen Saviour shines upon you!
> Let this place resound with joy,
> echoing the mighty song of all God's people!
>
> Lift up your hearts.
> **We lift them up to the Lord.**
>
> Let us give thanks to the Lord our God.
> **It is right to give him thanks and praise.**

---

*If the font is near the porch, a baptism during the Vigil service may take place either at a temporary font in front of the congregation or at the font near the porch, the congregation so turning that they can clearly see the baptism. If the former is done, the candle should be moved after the Vigil service to a place near the font in the porch; if the latter is done, the candle should be placed in front of the congregation when it is first brought in, but for the baptism it should be moved to a place near the font and remain there after the Vigil service.

The candle should be lit at all services until Pentecost and afterwards for all baptisms throughout the year.

It is truly right that with full hearts and minds and voices we should praise the unseen God, the all-powerful Father, and his only Son, our Lord Jesus Christ, who has ransomed us with his blood, and reconciled us to the Father.

For this is our Passover feast, when Christ, the true Lamb, is slain, whose blood consecrates the homes of all believers.

This is the night when first you saved our fathers: you freed the people of Israel from their slavery and led them dry-shod through the sea.

Most blessed of all nights, chosen by God to see Christ rising from the dead!

This is the night by whose power sin is purged; innocence restored to the fallen and joy to the mourners; hatred is vanquished; tyranny is laid low; harmony reigns.

This is the truly happy night on which heaven and earth are united and humanity is reconciled with God.

On this night, Holy Father, accept the light which we offer to your glory. Let it ever remind us that the Morning Star which has risen, never again to set, now shines clearly upon all the world.

22　A sermon may be preached.

23　If there is a Baptism service, it may take place now and may be completed by Confirmation.

Reaffirmation of Baptism

24 The congregation shall stand for the reaffirmation of the vows
and the prayer.
Before the reaffirmation of baptismal vows, the minister
addresses the congregation in the following or similar words:

> Dearly beloved: We too have been buried with Christ
> through baptism, so that we may rise with him to a new
> life. Now that we have completed the observance of
> Lent, let us renew the promises made in baptism when
> we rejected evil and promised to serve God faithfully in
> his holy catholic Church and in the world. And so:

> Do you repent of your sins?
> **I do.**

> Do you renounce evil?
> **I do.**

> Do you believe in God, the Father almighty, creator of
> heaven and earth?
> **I do.**

> Do you believe in Jesus Christ, his only Son, our Lord,
> who was born of the Virgin Mary, was crucified, died
> and was buried, rose from the dead, and is now seated
> at the right hand of the Father?
> **I do.**

> Do you believe in the Holy Spirit, the holy catholic Church,
> the communion of saints, the forgiveness of sins, the
> resurrection of the body, and life everlasting?
> **I do.**

Minister

Let us pray.

Lord Jesus Christ,
in your own appointed ordinance
you accept and seal your disciples
as members of your mystical body.
Let all who by baptism have been admitted
    into your holy Church
ever be faithful to their vows,
and live from now on as those who, being dead to sin,
are partakers of your risen power and glory;
for the honour of your holy name. **Amen.**

25 This prayer can be followed by a hymn, such as 'Ye Choirs of New Jerusalem'.

Thanksgiving for the Resurrection

26 A Thanksgiving for the Resurrection may follow, if there is no Eucharist.

Minister

Let us bless the Father, the Son and the Holy Spirit;
Let us praise and exalt him for ever.

All

Blessing and honour and glory and power be to him
who sits upon the throne and to the Lamb for ever and
ever.

Great and marvellous are your works, Lord God
    Almighty;
Just and true are your ways, King of saints;
All glorious your gifts, Spirit of life.

157

Blessing and glory and wisdom and thanksgiving and honour and power and might be to our God for ever and ever. Amen.

O give thanks to the Lord, for he is gracious:
and his mercy endures for ever.

Who has loved us from all eternity:
for his mercy endures for ever.

And remembered us when we were in trouble:
for his mercy endures for ever.

For us men and for our salvation he came down from
  heaven:
for his mercy endures for ever.

He became incarnate of the Virgin Mary by the power of
  the Holy Spirit, and was made man:
for his mercy endures for ever.

Who by his cross and passion has redeemed the world:
for his mercy endures for ever.

And has washed us from our sins in his own blood:
for his mercy endures for ever.

Who on the third day rose again:
for his mercy endures for ever.

And has given us the victory:
for his mercy endures for ever.

Who ascended into heaven:
for his mercy endures for ever.

And opened wide for us the everlasting doors:
for his mercy endures for ever.

Who is seated at the right hand of the Father:
for his mercy endures for ever.

And ever lives to make intercession for us:
for his mercy endures for ever.

**Glory to the Father, and to the Son,
and to the Holy Spirit:
as it was in the beginning, is now,
and shall be for ever. Amen.**

For the gift of his Spirit:
Blessed be Christ.

For the catholic Church:
Blessed be Christ.

For the means of grace:
Blessed be Christ.

For the hope of glory:
Blessed be Christ.

For the triumphs of his gospel:
Blessed be Christ.

For the lives of his saints:
Blessed be Christ.

In joy and in sorrow:
Blessed be Christ.

In life and in death:
Blessed be Christ.

Now and to the end of the ages:
Blessed be Christ.

All

Blessing and honour and thanksgiving and praise more
than we can utter, more than we can conceive, be to
you, O most adorable Trinity, Father, Son and Holy
Spirit, by all angels, all people, all creatures, for ever and
ever. Amen and Amen.

27 The eucharistic service continues from the Intercessions or the Offertory and is celebrated according to local custom. Further lections are not necessary.

28 If there is no eucharistic service following, this form of ending shall be used to conclude the service:

> The Lord be with you.
> **And with your spirit.**
>
> Let us bless the Lord.
> **Thanks be to God.**

Minister

> Now the God of peace, who brought again from the dead our Lord Jesus, that great shepherd of the sheep, through the blood of the everlasting covenant, make you perfect in every good work to do his will, working in you that which is well-pleasing in his sight, through Jesus Christ; to whom be glory for ever and ever. **Amen.**